Stress Relief Through Mindfulness:

Proven Methods Backed by Research

Evidence-Based Tools for a Calmer, Healthier You.

Cameron Dunk

Evidence Based Stress Management ©

Stress Relief Through Mindfulness: Proven Methods Backed by Research

Published by:
Evidence Based Stress Management
First published: July 17, 2025

ISBN: 978-1-7642369-3-5

For more information, visit: **www.ebsm.com.au**

Foreword

Stress Relief Through Mindfulness: Proven Methods Backed by Research explores the scientific foundations of mindfulness as a powerful tool for stress relief. Drawing from contemporary research in neuroscience, psychology, and medicine, it examines how mindfulness practices — such as mindful movement, breath awareness, and body scanning — affect brain function, hormonal balance, and emotional regulation. The book highlights key studies that demonstrate the physiological and psychological benefits of mindfulness, including reduced cortisol levels, improved cognitive flexibility, and enhanced resilience to stress.

By bridging ancient contemplative traditions with modern empirical evidence, this guide offers you a clear understanding of how and why mindfulness works. Designed for both newcomers and experienced practitioners, it provides practical insights and evidence-based strategies to cultivate mindfulness and foster long-term well-being.

Contents

Introduction

In a world that moves faster by the day, stress has become a near-constant companion for many. From the pressures of work and relationships to the endless stream of digital distractions, our minds are often pulled in countless directions, leaving us feeling overwhelmed and disconnected. Amid this chaos, mindfulness offers a quiet revolution — a way to reclaim calm, clarity, and control.

But mindfulness is more than just a buzzword or a fleeting wellness trend. It is a practice rooted in centuries of contemplative tradition and increasingly validated by modern science. Neuroscientists, psychologists, and medical researchers have begun to uncover how mindfulness affects the brain, body, and behaviour, revealing its profound potential to reduce stress, enhance emotional regulation, and improve overall well-being.

This book explores the intersection of ancient wisdom and contemporary research. We'll delve into how mindfulness works, what happens in the brain when practicing mindfulness, and why simple methods like focused breathing or body scans can lead to measurable changes in stress levels. Whether you're a curious beginner or a seasoned practitioner, this guide will help you understand the "why" behind the "how" — empowering you to integrate mindfulness into your life with purpose and confidence.

While the methods we discuss are thorough and effective, they are not an exhaustive list. It is crucial to consult a medical professional before undertaking any new stress management techniques, especially if you are experiencing significant stress. A healthcare provider can offer personalized advice and ensure that the methods you choose are safe and appropriate for your specific circumstances.

What is Mindfulness?

Mindfulness is the intentional, non-judgmental awareness of the present moment. It involves paying attention to your thoughts, emotions, bodily sensations, and environment with openness and curiosity.

This definition is widely attributed to Jon Kabat-Zinn, who developed the Mindfulness-Based Stress Reduction (MBSR) program at the University of Massachusetts Medical School in the late 1970s.

"Mindfulness means paying attention in a particular way: on purpose, in the present moment, and non-judgmentally."
— *Jon Kabat-Zinn*

The key components of mindfulness are:

1) **Attention:** Directing your focus deliberately to what is happening right now. For example, noticing the sensation of your breath entering and leaving your nostrils.

2) **Awareness:** Observing your internal and external experiences without becoming entangled in them. For example, recognising that you're feeling anxious without trying to suppress or fix it.

3) **Acceptance:** Allowing experiences to be as they are, without judgement or resistance. For example, letting a difficult emotion arise and pass without labelling it as 'bad' or trying to push it away.

Imagine you're stuck in traffic and running late. A non-mindful reaction might involve:

- Ruminating about being late.

- Blaming yourself or others.

- Feeling overwhelmed.

A mindful response would involve:

- Noticing the tension in your body.

- Acknowledging your frustration without judgment.

- Bringing your attention to your breath or surroundings.

- Choosing a calm response.

Understanding Stress

Stress is a physiological and psychological response to perceived challenges or threats. While acute stress can be adaptive – enhancing alertness and performance – chronic stress can lead to serious health consequences.

"Stress can be brief, situational, and a positive force motivating performance, but if experienced over an extended period of time it can become chronic stress, which negatively impacts health and well-being" (American Psychological Association, 2023).

Impact of Stress on Health

While stress is a natural part of life, chronic stress can have profound effects on both physical and mental health. These effects include:

1) **Cardiovascular Health:** Chronic stress can contribute to high blood pressure, inflammation, and increased risk of heart disease (Steptoe & Kivimäki, 2012).

2) **Immune Function:** Stress can suppress immune responses, making the body more vulnerable to infections and slowing recovery (Segerstrom & Miller, 2004).

3) **Endocrine and Metabolic Effects:** Stress can activate the hypothalamic-pituitary-adrenal (HPA) axis, leading to prolonged cortisol secretion, which disrupts metabolism and increases the risk of obesity and diabetes (Chrousos, 2009).

4) **Mental Health:** Stress is a major contributor to anxiety, depression, and cognitive decline. It affects brain regions involved in emotion regulation and memory (Lupien, McEwen, Gunnar, & Heim, 2009).

Why Mindfulness is a Powerful Tool for Stress Management

Mindfulness is not just a relaxation technique — it is a scientifically validated approach that transforms how the brain and body respond to stress. By cultivating present-moment awareness and acceptance, mindfulness empowers you to navigate life's challenges with greater resilience and well-being.

The benefits of mindfulness in stress management include:

1) **Reduction in Physiological Stress Responses:** Mindfulness practices, such as meditation and breath awareness, reduce activation of the hypothalamic-pituitary-adrenal (HPA) axis, which governs the body's stress response. This leads to lower levels of cortisol, the primary stress hormone (American Psychological Association, 2019).

2) **Enhancing Emotional Regulation:** Mindfulness strengthens the prefrontal cortex, which is responsible for executive function and emotion regulation, while reducing activity in the amygdala, the brain's fear centre (American Psychological Association, 2019).

3) **Improvement of Psychological Resilience:** Mindfulness fosters a non-judgmental awareness of thoughts and feelings, which helps you respond to stressors with greater clarity and calmness rather than automatic reactivity (American Psychological Association, 2019).

4) **Supporting Long-Term Mental Health:** Mindfulness-Based Stress Reduction (MBSR) and Mindfulness-Based Cognitive Therapy (MBCT) have been shown to prevent relapse in individuals with recurrent depression and to improve overall well-being (American Psychological Association, 2019).

Part I: Understanding the Foundations

Chapter 1

The Science of Stress

Before we can appreciate how mindfulness alleviates stress, it's essential to first understand what stress actually is. By grasping the mechanisms behind stress — how it affects our brain, body, and behaviour — we lay the groundwork for understanding how mindfulness intervenes. This foundational knowledge allows us to see mindfulness not as a vague concept, but as a scientifically grounded method for calming the stress response and restoring balance. You can find a more thorough definition of stress and its mechanisms in our book '*Managing Stress: An Evidence Based Guide*'.

What is Stress?

Stress is the body's natural response to any demand or threat, whether real or perceived. It activates a cascade of physiological changes — commonly known as the "fight-or-flight" response — that prepare the body to respond to danger. This response is mediated by the hypothalamic-pituitary-adrenal (HPA) axis, which releases stress hormones such as cortisol and adrenaline (American Psychological Association, 2023).

Acute Stress

Acute stress is short-term and typically arises in response to immediate challenges or perceived threats. It can be beneficial in small doses, enhancing alertness, motivation, and performance. Physiological effects include increased heart rate, rapid breathing, muscle tension, and heightened senses. This may be due to things such as taking an exam or public speaking. Once the threat passes, the body returns to baseline relatively quickly.

Chronic Stress

Chronic stress occurs when stressors persist over an extended period, and the body remains in a heightened state. This prolonged activation of the stress response system can lead to wear and tear on the body and brain. It may arise due to ongoing financial difficulties, caregiving for a chronically ill loved one, or long-term job insecurity.

Chronic stress can have the following health impacts on your body:

- **Cardiovascular:** Increased risk of hypertension, heart disease, and stroke.

- **Musculoskeletal:** Persistent muscle tension leading to headaches and chronic pain.
- **Immune:** Suppressed immune function, increasing susceptibility to illness.
- **Mental Health:** Higher risk of anxiety, depression, and cognitive decline.

The Biological Mechanisms of Stress

When the brain perceives a threat, the stress response is a highly coordinated biological process involving the Sympathetic Nervous System (SNS), Hypothalamic-Pituitary-Adrenal (HPA) axis, cortisol, Parasympathetic Nervous System (PNS), and Enteric Nervous System (ENS). While these systems are essential for survival, chronic activation can lead to significant health issues. Understanding these mechanisms is key to developing effective stress management strategies.

1) Sympathetic Nervous System (SNS)

The SNS is the first responder in the stress response, initiating the "fight-or-flight" reaction.

- **Function:** The amygdala signals the hypothalamus, which activates the SNS. This leads to the release of adrenaline and noradrenaline from the adrenal medulla (Kandel et al., 2013).

- **Stress Impact:** Increased heart rate, blood pressure, respiration, pupil dilation, and energy mobilization. Blood is redirected from the digestive system to muscles and the brain (Kandel et al., 2013).

2) Hypothalamic-Pituitary-Adrenal (HPA) Axis

The HPA axis provides a slower, sustained response to stress.

- **Step 1:** The hypothalamus releases corticotropin-releasing hormone (CRH) (Kandel et al., 2013).

- **Step 2:** CRH stimulates the pituitary gland to release adrenocorticotropic hormone (ACTH) (Kandel et al., 2013).

- **Step 3:** ACTH prompts the adrenal cortex to release cortisol, the primary stress hormone (Kandel et al., 2013).

3) Cortisol

Cortisol helps maintain energy supply by increasing glucose availability, suppressing non-essential functions (e.g. digestion, reproduction), and modulating immune responses (Kandel et al., 2013).

- **Short-Term Effects:** Enhances alertness and energy.

- **Long-Term Effects:** Chronic elevation can impair immune function, increase abdominal fat, and contribute to anxiety and depression (Kandel et al., 2013).

4) Parasympathetic Nervous System (PNS)

The PNS is the counterpart to the SNS and is responsible for the "rest-and-digest" response.

- **Function:** After the threat passes, the PNS helps return the body to normal by slowing the heart rate, reducing blood pressure, and resuming digestion (Kandel et al., 2013).

- **Stress Impact:** Stress can suppress the activity of the parasympathetic nervous system, reducing its ability to promote relaxation and recovery. This can lead to prolonged activation of the body's stress response and contribute to physical and mental health issues over time (Kandel et al., 2013).

5) Enteric Nervous System (ENS)

The ENS, often called the "second brain," governs the gastrointestinal system and is deeply influenced by stress.

- **Function:** Regulates digestion, enzyme secretion, and gut motility (Bankenahally & Krovvidi, 2016).

- **Stress Impact:** Stress can disrupt ENS function, leading to gastrointestinal issues such as irritable bowel syndrome (IBS), nausea, and appetite changes (Bankenahally & Krovvidi, 2016).

Effects of Stress on the Brain and Body

Stress affects nearly every system in the body and brain. While acute stress can be adaptive, chronic stress leads to structural and functional changes that increase vulnerability to disease. Understanding these mechanisms is essential for prevention and treatment.

Effects of stress on the brain include:

- **Hippocampus (Memory and Learning):** Chronic stress impairs the hippocampus, a region essential for memory consolidation and spatial navigation. Elevated cortisol levels reduce neurogenesis and synaptic plasticity, leading to memory deficits (McEwen, 2007).

- **Amygdala (Emotion and Fear):** Stress enhances amygdala activity, increasing emotional reactivity and fear conditioning. This can heighten anxiety and sensitivity to future stressors (Vyas, Mitra, Shankaranarayana, & Chattarji 2002).

- **Prefrontal Cortex (Executive Function):** The prefrontal cortex, responsible for decision-making and impulse control, is weakened by chronic stress, leading to poor judgment and emotional dysregulation (Arnsten, 2009).

Effects of stress on the body include:

- **Cardiovascular System:** Stress increases heart rate and blood pressure, contributing to hypertension and cardiovascular disease (Steptoe & Kivimäki, 2012).

- **Immune System:** Chronic stress suppresses immune function, reducing the body's ability to fight infections and heal wounds (Segerstrom & Miller, 2004).

- **Gastrointestinal System:** Stress disrupts gut motility and microbiota, contributing to conditions like irritable bowel syndrome (IBS) (Mayer, 2011).

- **Endocrine System:** Stress activates the HPA axis, leading to prolonged cortisol release, which can disrupt metabolism and increase the risk of obesity and diabetes (Chrousos, 2009).

Stress-Related Disorders

Stress-related disorders are psychological and physiological conditions that arise from prolonged or intense exposure to stress. These disorders involve dysregulation of the hypothalamic-pituitary-adrenal (HPA) axis, autonomic nervous system, and neurotransmitter systems, leading to changes in mood, cognition, and physical health.

Post-Traumatic Stress Disorder (PTSD)

PTSD is a psychiatric disorder that can occur after experiencing or witnessing a traumatic event. It is characterized by intrusive memories, hyperarousal, avoidance behaviours, and negative alterations in mood and cognition. PTSD is associated with hyperactivity of the amygdala, reduced volume of the hippocampus, and impaired regulation by the prefrontal cortex. Bremner et al. (1995) found that individuals with PTSD had an 8% smaller hippocampal volume compared to individuals without PTSD, suggesting these findings are stress-induced.

Generalized Anxiety Disorder (GAD)

GAD involves excessive, uncontrollable worry about various aspects of life. It is often accompanied by physical symptoms such as muscle tension, restlessness, and sleep disturbances. Dysregulation of the HPA axis and heightened sympathetic nervous system activity are common in GAD. Thayer et al. (2012) reported that individuals with anxiety disorders show reduced heart rate variability, indicating impaired parasympathetic regulation.

Major Depressive Disorder (MDD)

Chronic stress is a major risk factor for depression. MDD is characterized by persistent low mood, anhedonia, fatigue, and cognitive impairments. Elevated cortisol levels, reduced hippocampal volume, and altered serotonin and dopamine signalling are implicated. Sapolsky (2000) demonstrated that chronic stress leads to hippocampal atrophy and impaired neurogenesis, contributing to depressive symptoms.

Adjustment Disorder

This condition occurs when an individual has difficulty coping with a significant life change or stressor, leading to emotional or behavioural symptoms. While less studied, adjustment disorders may involve transient dysregulation of stress response systems. Research suggests that early intervention and stress management can prevent progression to more severe disorders (Casey & Bailey, 2013).

Chapter 2

What is Mindfulness?

Mindfulness has deep roots in Buddhist philosophy, where it is part of a broader ethical and spiritual path. While modern adaptations have made it accessible in secular contexts, understanding its historical and cultural origins enriches its practice and application.

Historical Roots

Buddhist Foundations

Mindfulness, or "sati" in Pāli, is a central concept in Theravāda Buddhism. It is one of the Seven Factors of Enlightenment and a key component of the Noble Eightfold Path. It refers to the quality of mind that observes phenomena as they are, without attachment or aversion.

The Satipaṭṭhāna Sutta (Foundations of Mindfulness) outlines four domains of mindfulness: the body, feelings, mind, and mental objects. These practices are intended to cultivate insight (vipassanā) and ultimately lead to liberation from suffering (Khong, 2021).

Mindfulness in Other Eastern Traditions

While Buddhism is the most cited origin of mindfulness, similar practices appear in Hinduism, Taoism, and Confucianism:

- **Hinduism:** Practices such as Dhyāna (meditation) and Pratyāhāra (withdrawal of the senses) in the Yoga Sūtras of Patañjali parallel mindfulness in their emphasis on focused attention and inner awareness.
- **Taoism:** Emphasizes harmony with the Tao (the Way), often cultivated through meditative stillness and attentiveness to the present moment.
- **Confucianism:** Encourages self-cultivation and reflection, which align with the introspective aspects of mindfulness.

The Modern Definition of Mindfulness

Jon Kabat-Zinn, a molecular biologist and meditation practitioner, introduced mindfulness into Western clinical settings in the late 1970s. He defined mindfulness as:

"Paying attention in a particular way: on purpose, in the present moment, and nonjudgmentally" (Kabat-Zinn, 2003).

This definition emphasizes three core elements:

1) **Intentionality:** mindfulness is a deliberate act of attention.

2) **Present-Moment Focus:** attention is anchored in the here and now.

3) **Non-Judgmental Awareness:** experiences are observed without labelling them as good or bad.

Mindfulness-Based Stress Reduction (MBSR)

Kabat-Zinn developed the **MBSR** program at the University of Massachusetts Medical School in 1979. Its goal is to cultivate awareness and reduce reactivity to stress, pain, and illness (Kabat-Zinn, 2003). It is an 8-week, evidence-based intervention that integrates:

- Body scan meditation
- Mindful breathing
- Hatha yoga
- Sitting and walking meditation
- Informal mindfulness in daily life

The Neuroscience of Mindfulness

Mindfulness practice leads to measurable changes in brain structure and function, particularly in areas involved in attention regulation, emotional processing, and self-referential thinking.

These include:

1) Default Mode Network (DMN)

The DMN is a network of brain regions — including the medial prefrontal cortex and posterior cingulate cortex — that is active during rest and mind-wandering. It is associated with self-referential processing, rumination, and autobiographical memory.

Mindfulness meditation reduces activity in the DMN, which is often overactive in individuals with anxiety and depression. This reduction is associated with decreased rumination and improved present-moment awareness (Wheeler, Arnkoff, & Glass, 2017).

2) Prefrontal Cortex (PFC)

The PFC is responsible for executive functions such as attention, decision-making, and emotion regulation. Mindfulness enhances both the structure (e.g. cortical thickness) and function (e.g. activation) of the PFC (Wheeler, Arnkoff, & Glass, 2017). This supports improved cognitive control and emotional resilience.

3) Amygdala

The amygdala is a key structure in the brain's fear and emotion processing system. It plays a central role in detecting threats and initiating the stress response. Mindfulness practice is associated with reduced amygdala reactivity to emotional stimuli and decreased amygdala volume over time (Wheeler, Arnkoff, & Glass, 2017).

Chapter 3

Evidence-Based Benefits of Mindfulness

Key Findings from Research on Mindfulness

There are many academic studies that provide robust evidence that mindfulness is a powerful tool for reducing stress, enhancing emotional regulation, and improving overall well-being. The benefits are observed across diverse populations and are supported by both psychological and biological measures.

1) Cognitive and Attentional Benefits

A comprehensive meta-analysis by Sumantry and Stewart (2021) analysed 87 studies on mindfulness and attention. It found that mindfulness practices — especially focused attention (FA) and open monitoring (OM) — significantly improved various aspects of attention, including alerting, executive control, and cognitive inhibition. Participants who practiced mindfulness showed better performance on tasks requiring sustained attention and cognitive flexibility.

2) Emotional Regulation and Psychological Well-Being

Davis and Hayes (2012) reviewed empirical studies showing that mindfulness enhances emotional regulation, reduces rumination, and increases self-awareness. These effects contribute to lower levels of anxiety, depression, and emotional reactivity. Therapists who practiced mindfulness reported greater emotional resilience and improved therapeutic outcomes with clients.

3) Clinical Applications and Mental Health

Mindfulness-Based Stress Reduction (MBSR) and Mindfulness-Based Cognitive Therapy (MBCT) have been shown to be effective in treating a range of psychological disorders, including depression, anxiety, PTSD, and chronic pain. Grossman et al. (2004) found that MBSR significantly reduced stress and improved quality of life across both clinical and non-clinical populations.

4) Neurobiological Changes

Mindfulness has been linked to structural and functional changes in the brain, including increased gray matter density in the hippocampus and prefrontal cortex, and reduced activity in the amygdala. Davidson et al. (2003) found that participants in an 8-week MBSR program showed increased left-sided anterior brain activation (associated with positive affect) and improved immune function.

Mindfulness and Mental Health

Mindfulness is a powerful, evidence-based approach for managing a range of mental health conditions. Its benefits are supported by neurobiological, psychological, and behavioural research, making it a valuable tool in both clinical and non-clinical settings.

Anxiety

Mindfulness practices can help reduce anxiety by enhancing emotional regulation and decreasing reactivity to stressors. They reduce activity in the amygdala and increases connectivity with the prefrontal cortex, improving regulation of fear and anxiety responses. Strohmaier, Jones, and Cane (2021) found that both short (5-minute) and long (20-minute) mindfulness practices significantly reduced anxiety levels in healthy adults, with shorter practices showing even greater effects for beginners.

Depression

Mindfulness reduces rumination and increases cognitive flexibility, helping you disengage from negative thought patterns. Mindfulness-Based Cognitive Therapy (MBCT) and Mindfulness-Based Stress Reduction (MBSR) have been shown to reduce depressive symptoms and prevent relapse in individuals with recurrent depression. Khoury et al. (2015)

found that mindfulness-based interventions significantly reduced symptoms of depression, with effect sizes comparable to traditional cognitive behavioural therapy.

Post-Traumatic Stress Disorder (PTSD)

Mindfulness enhances interoceptive awareness and reduces the intensity of trauma-related triggers through exposure and acceptance. This can help individuals with PTSD by fostering a nonjudgmental awareness of traumatic memories and bodily sensations, reducing avoidance and hyperarousal. Studies have shown that mindfulness-based interventions reduce PTSD symptoms in veterans and trauma survivors by improving emotion regulation and decreasing physiological reactivity (Aldbyani, 2025).

Burnout

Mindfulness is increasingly used to address burnout, especially among healthcare professionals, educators, and caregivers. It can interrupt the chronic stress cycle by activating the parasympathetic nervous system and reducing cortisol levels. This can improve resilience, emotional regulation, and self-compassion. Aldbyani (2025) found that mindfulness meditation significantly reduced stress, anxiety, and depression among university students, while also improving psychological well-being and emotion regulation

Cognitive and Emotional Regulation and Mindfulness

Mindfulness enhances both cognitive and emotional regulation through neurobiological and psychological mechanisms. These improvements contribute to greater mental clarity, emotional resilience, and overall well-being.

Cognitive Regulation

Mindfulness enhances cognitive regulation by improving attention control, working memory, and executive functioning. These improvements help you manage distractions, sustain focus, and respond more adaptively to stressors. McBride and Greeson (2021) found that higher trait mindfulness was associated with better self-reported cognitive functioning in college students. This relationship was mediated by lower perceived stress, suggesting that mindfulness supports cognition by reducing stress-related interference.

Emotional Regulation

Mindfulness fosters emotional regulation by increasing awareness of emotional states and reducing automatic, reactive responses. It can reduce activity in the amygdala (the brain's fear centre) and increases connectivity with the prefrontal cortex, enhancing top-down regulation of emotions. This can encourage acceptance and nonjudgmental observation of emotions, which helps you respond more skilfully. Jones (2018) highlighted that mindfulness meditation helps individuals observe aversive stimuli objectively, reducing emotional attachment and reactivity.

Integration of Cognitive and Emotional Regulation

Mindfulness integrates cognitive and emotional regulation by training you to monitor your internal experiences (thoughts, emotions, sensations) with clarity and equanimity. This dual regulation supports better decision-making, stress management, and interpersonal functioning (Aldbyani, 2025).

Physical health outcomes from Mindfulness

Mindfulness has measurable effects on physical health, including enhanced immune function, lower blood pressure, reduced chronic pain, and improved sleep. These benefits are mediated by changes in stress physiology, autonomic regulation, and inflammation.

Immune Function

Mindfulness meditation has been shown to positively influence immune system functioning by reducing inflammation and enhancing immune cell activity. Davidson et al. (2003) found that participants in an 8-week Mindfulness-Based Stress Reduction (MBSR) program showed increased antibody production in response to an influenza vaccine, along with increased left-sided anterior brain activation associated with positive affect. Furthermore, Black and Slavich (2016) concluded that mindfulness meditation is associated with reductions in pro-inflammatory cytokines and improvements in immune cell gene expression.

Blood Pressure and Cardiovascular Health

Mindfulness practices can help reduce systolic and diastolic blood pressure, likely through mechanisms involving reduced sympathetic nervous system activity and improved autonomic regulation. Singh, Mishra, and Singh (2022) found that both mindfulness and transcendental meditation produced clinically significant reductions in blood pressure among individuals with hypertension. Furthermore, mindfulness has been found to reduce stress-induced activation of the hypothalamic-pituitary-adrenal (HPA) axis and sympathetic nervous system, promoting parasympathetic (rest-and-digest) activity (Pascoe, Thompson, Jenkins, & Ski, 2017).

Other Physical Health Outcomes

- **Chronic Pain:** Mindfulness can help you reframe your relationship with pain, reducing the emotional and cognitive burden of chronic pain conditions. MBSR has been shown to reduce pain intensity and improve quality of life in patients with fibromyalgia, arthritis, and lower back pain (Davidson et al., 2003).

- **Sleep Quality:** Mindfulness can improve sleep by reducing cognitive arousal and promoting relaxation. Studies show that mindfulness interventions improve sleep onset latency, sleep efficiency, and overall sleep quality in individuals with insomnia and stress-related sleep disturbances (Davidson et al., 2003).

Part II: Core Mindfulness Techniques

We will now explore the core techniques of mindfulness through the lens of neuroscience and psychology, revealing how simple shifts in attention and awareness can lead to profound changes in well-being. It's important to remember that mindfulness is not a one-size-fits-all solution. Each technique offers unique benefits, but not every method will resonate with every individual. The key is to explore, experiment, and find what works best for you.

Although these approaches are comprehensive and effective, they do not represent every possible option. It's important to speak with a medical professional before trying any new stress management strategies, particularly if you're dealing with high levels of stress. A healthcare provider can offer tailored guidance and help ensure that the techniques you choose are safe and suitable for your individual needs.

Chapter 4

Mindful Breathing

Mindful breathing is a foundational mindfulness practice that involves focusing attention on the natural rhythm of the breath. It is often used as a gateway to deeper mindfulness and meditation practices. Scientifically, its stress-reducing effects are largely attributed to its ability to activate the parasympathetic nervous system (PNS) — the branch of the autonomic nervous system responsible for the "rest and digest" response.

How it Works

- You bring attention to the inhalation and exhalation of the breath, often focusing on sensations at the nostrils, chest, or abdomen.

- When the mind wanders, you gently return your attention to the breath without judgment.

- This process cultivates present-moment awareness, attentional control, and emotional regulation.

1) **Counting the Breath:** Inhale and exhale while silently counting (e.g. "one" on the inhale, "two" on the exhale, up to ten, then repeat). This helps anchor attention and reduces mental chatter.

2) **Box Breathing (Four-Square Breathing):** Inhale for 4 seconds → Hold for 4 seconds → Exhale for 4 seconds → Hold for 4 seconds. This if often used by athletes and military personnel to manage stress and enhance focus.

3) **Extended Exhalation:** Inhale for 4 seconds, exhale for 6–8 seconds. This activates the parasympathetic nervous system, promoting relaxation.

4) **Breath Awareness with Labelling:** Mentally label the breath as "in" and "out" or "rising" and "falling." This can enhance metacognitive awareness and reduce identification with thoughts.

The Scientific Rationale Behind Mindful Breathing

When we engage in slow, deep breathing — especially with prolonged exhalation — we stimulate the vagus nerve, which plays a central role in parasympathetic activation (Richer et al., 2022). This can lead to:

- Decreased heart rate.
- Lower blood pressure.
- Reduced respiratory rate.

- Increased heart rate variability (HRV), a marker of autonomic flexibility and resilience.

Scientific Support

- Zeidan et al. (2010) found that brief mindfulness meditation, including breath-focused attention, improved working memory and sustained attention.
- Arch and Craske (2006) showed that mindful breathing reduced emotional reactivity to distressing images compared to distraction techniques.
- Taren et al. (2015) demonstrated that mindfulness training reduced amygdala reactivity and increased connectivity with the prefrontal cortex, supporting better stress regulation.
- Creswell et al. (2016) found that mindfulness-based interventions lowered blood pressure and cortisol levels, especially when breath awareness was emphasized.

Common Challenges in Mindful Breathing and How to Overcome Them

Mindful breathing is simple but not always easy. Common challenges — like distraction, restlessness, and self-judgment — are part of the learning process. With consistent practice and compassionate awareness, these obstacles become opportunities for growth.

1) **Mind Wandering:** One of the most frequently reported difficulties is the tendency for the mind to wander during practice — thinking about the past, future, or unrelated topics. To resolve this, gently acknowledge the distraction without judgment and return attention to the breath. This redirection is not a failure but a core part of the practice. Mind wandering is a natural cognitive process. Studies show that mindfulness training improves meta-awareness and attentional control, helping you notice and redirect wandering thoughts more effectively (American Psychological Association, 2019).

2) **Impatience or Restlessness:** Beginners often feel bored, restless, or impatient, especially during longer sessions. This can be resolved by starting shorter sessions (2–5 minutes) and gradually increasing duration. Incorporating movement-based mindfulness (e.g. walking meditation) to channel restlessness constructively can also help. Mindfulness-based interventions like MBSR emphasize gradual exposure and acceptance of discomfort, which builds tolerance and resilience over time (American Psychological Association, 2019).

3) **Difficulty Focusing on the Breath:** Some individuals struggle to locate or stay with the breath, especially if they are anxious or distracted. This can be resolved using breath-counting or labelling each breath ("in" and "out") to anchor attention. Alternatively, focus on the rise and fall of the abdomen or the sound of breathing. Structured breath awareness techniques enhance interoceptive awareness and reduce cognitive load, making it easier to maintain focus (American Psychological Association, 2019).

4) **Judgement and Self-Criticism:** You may judge yourself for "not doing it right" or for being distracted. To resolve this, practice self-compassion. Remind yourself that mindfulness is about observing without judgment. Each return to the breath is a moment of mindfulness. Acceptance is a core component of mindfulness. Studies show that cultivating a non-judgmental attitude reduces emotional reactivity and increases adherence to practice (American Psychological Association, 2019).

5) **Physical Discomfort:** Sitting still can lead to discomfort in the back, legs, or shoulders. To resolve this, adjust posture, use cushions or chairs, or try lying down or walking meditation. Mindfulness includes awareness of discomfort without resistance. Mindfulness training

improves pain tolerance and reduces the emotional impact of discomfort by changing the way the brain processes pain signals (American Psychological Association, 2019).

Mindful Breathing: A Step-By-Step-Guide

1) Find a Comfortable Position

- Sit upright in a chair or on a cushion with your spine straight but not stiff.
- Rest your hands on your lap or knees.
- Gently close your eyes or lower your gaze.

"Allow your body to settle. Feel the support of the ground beneath you."

2) Bring Awareness to the Breath

- Begin by noticing your breath just as it is — no need to change it.
- Observe the natural rhythm of your inhalation and exhalation.

"Notice where you feel the breath most clearly — in your nose, chest, or belly."

3) Focus on the Sensation of Breathing

- Direct your attention to the in-breath and out-breath.
- You might silently say "in" as you inhale and "out" as you exhale.

"Feel the air entering your nostrils... and leaving your body. Let your breath anchor you in the present moment."

4) Acknowledge Distractions

- When your mind wanders (which it will), gently notice it without judgment.
- Then, return your attention to the breath.

"If thoughts arise, acknowledge them - 'thinking' — and gently return to the breath."

5) Deepen the Breath (Optional)

- If you feel comfortable, begin to slightly lengthen your exhalation.
- Try inhaling for 4 seconds and exhaling for 6 seconds.

"With each exhale, allow your body to soften and release tension."

6) Close the Practice

- After a few minutes, bring your awareness back to your body and surroundings.
- Gently wiggle your fingers and toes.
- Open your eyes when you're ready.

"Take a moment to notice how you feel. Carry this awareness with you into the rest of your day."

Suggested Duration

- Beginners: 3–5 minutes.

- Intermediate: 10–15 minutes.

- Advanced: 20+ minutes.

Chapter 5

Body Scan Meditation

Body scan meditation is a somatically oriented mindfulness practice that involves systematically directing attention to different parts of the body, usually from head to toe or vice versa. The goal is to cultivate nonjudgmental awareness of bodily sensations, tension, and areas of discomfort or ease. It is a core component of Mindfulness-Based Stress Reduction (MBSR) and Mindfulness-Based Cognitive Therapy (MBCT) programs.

Psychological and Physiological benefits

1) Enhanced Interoceptive Awareness

Body scan meditation can improve awareness of internal bodily states, which is linked to better emotional regulation and self-awareness. Dambrun et al. (2019) found that body scan meditation significantly increased feelings of inner-body awareness, harmony, and unified consciousness, which mediated increases in happiness.

2) Reduced Stress and Anxiety

By shifting attention from ruminative thoughts to bodily sensations, body scan meditation can help reduce physiological arousal and emotional reactivity. Studies show that body scan meditation reduces activity in the default mode network (DMN), which is associated with mind-wandering and stress (American Psychological Association, 2019).

3) Improved Sleep and Relaxation

Practicing body scan before bed can reduce insomnia symptoms and promote deeper sleep by calming the nervous system. Individuals with chronic insomnia reported improved sleep quality after incorporating body scan meditation into their nightly routine (Ong, Shapiro, & Manber, 2008).

Benefits for Somatic Awareness and Stress Reduction

Somatic Awareness – Enhanced Interoceptive Awareness

Body scan meditation improves interoception – the ability to perceive internal bodily sensations. This heightened awareness helps individuals detect subtle physical cues related to stress, tension, or emotional states. Dreeben, Mamberg, and Salmon (2013) describes the body scan as a practice that fosters nonjudgmental awareness of bodily sensations, which can lead to greater self-regulation and emotional insight. For example, you are practicing body scan and notice tightness in your shoulders and consciously release it, preventing the buildup of chronic tension.

Stress Reduction – Downregulation of the Stress Response

By shifting attention from ruminative thoughts to present-moment bodily sensations, body scan meditation helps reduce sympathetic nervous system activity and activate the parasympathetic nervous system, promoting relaxation. The body scan has been shown to reduce physiological markers of stress, such as heart rate and cortisol levels, and improve psychological outcomes in individuals with anxiety, depression, and chronic pain (Dreeben, Mamberg, & Salmon, 2013). Participants in MBSR programs often report feeling calmer and more grounded after body scan sessions, even during periods of high stress (Dreeben, Mamberg, & Salmon, 2013).

Body Scan Meditation: Step-by-Step-Guide

1) Settle into a Comfortable Position

- Lie down on your back or sit in a chair with your spine straight and body relaxed.
- Let your arms rest by your sides or on your lap.
- Close your eyes gently or soften your gaze.

"Allow your body to be still. Feel the support of the ground or chair beneath you."

2) Begin with the Breath

- Bring your attention to your breathing.
- Notice the natural rhythm of your inhale and exhale.
- Use the breath to anchor your awareness in the present moment.

"Feel the rise and fall of your belly or chest with each breath."

3) Focus on the Top of the Head

- Begin the scan at the crown of your head.
- Notice any sensations — tingling, warmth, pressure, or even absence of sensation.
- Simply observe without trying to change anything.

4) Move Downward Gradually

Continue scanning the body in small sections. Spend 15-30 seconds on each area:

- Forehead, eyes, cheeks, jaw (release tension).
- Neck and shoulders (notice tightness or heaviness).
- Arms, hands, and fingers (feel temperature or pulse).
- Chest and upper back (observe breath movement).
- Abdomen and lower back (notice digestion or tension).
- Hips and pelvis (feel contact with the surface).
- Thighs, knees, calves (observe heaviness or lightness).

- Ankles, feet, and toes (notice sensations at the soles).

"If you notice discomfort, acknowledge it with kindness and move on."

5) Acknowledge Distractions

- If your mind wanders, gently bring it back to the body part you were focusing on.
- Use the breath as a gentle guide back to the present.

6) Complete the Scan

- After reaching the feet, expand your awareness to include the entire body.
- Notice how your body feels as a whole — connected, grounded, and present.

"Rest in this full-body awareness for a few breaths."

7) Gently Transition

- Wiggle your fingers and toes.
- Open your eyes slowly.
- Take a moment to notice how you feel before moving on with your day.

Suggested Duration

- Beginners: 5-10 minutes.
- Intermediate: 15-30 minutes.
- Advanced: 30-45 minutes.

Chapter 6
Mindful Movement

Mindful Movement and Stress Management

Mindful movement refers to physical activities performed with intentional awareness of bodily sensations, breath, and mental states. Common forms include yoga, tai chi, and qigong. These practices integrate mindfulness principles — such as present-moment awareness and non-judgmental observation — with physical movement, offering a holistic approach to stress management.

Mindful movement reduces stress through several interrelated mechanisms:

- **Physiological Regulation:** It activates the parasympathetic nervous system, reducing heart rate and cortisol levels (Sanada et al., 2016).

- **Cognitive-Emotional Regulation:** It enhances awareness of thoughts and emotions, allowing for more adaptive responses to stress (Sanada et al., 2016).

- **Embodied Awareness:** By focusing on bodily sensations, individuals become more attuned to early signs of stress and can intervene sooner (Sanada et al., 2016).

Mindful Movement Practices

Yoga

Yoga is one of the most researched forms of mindful movement. It integrates physical postures (asanas), breath control (pranayama), and meditation. It is widely used in clinical and wellness settings to reduce stress and improve emotional regulation. Yoga activates the parasympathetic nervous system, reduces cortisol levels, and enhances interoceptive awareness — our ability to perceive internal bodily sensations — which is linked to better emotional regulation (American Psychological Association, 2019).

Studies show that regular yoga practice can reduce perceived stress, anxiety, and depression. It can also improve sleep and emotional resilience. Davis et al. (2019) notes that yoga, as part of mindfulness-based stress reduction (MBSR), is effective in improving both mental and physical health.

Tai Chi and Qigong

Tai Chi is a traditional Chinese practice that combines slow, flowing movements with breath awareness and focused attention. It is often described as "meditation in motion." Tai

Chi improves heart rate variability (HRV), a marker of autonomic nervous system balance, and enhances interoceptive sensibility, which mediates reductions in anxiety and stress (Shen et al., 2023).

Qigong (pronounced chee-gong) is a holistic practice rooted in Traditional Chinese Medicine that integrates gentle movement, controlled breathing, and focused intention to cultivate and balance the body's vital energy, or qi. Studies have demonstrated that regular Qigong practice can lead to significant reductions in cortisol levels, the body's primary stress hormone, and improvements in psychological measures of stress, anxiety, and depression (Larkey et al., 2009). These effects are believed to result from Qigong's ability to activate the parasympathetic nervous system, promoting relaxation and counteracting the physiological impacts of chronic stress (Chow, Dorcas, & Siu, 2012).

Mindfulness-Based Stress Reduction (MBSR)

MBSR programs often incorporate the above practices and other mindful movement practices. These programs have been shown to reduce stress, anxiety, and depression across diverse populations. According to Glazer and Gasser (2016), MBSR's inclusion of mindful movement is key to its effectiveness in stress management.

For example, walking meditation is commonly practiced in MBSR programs. When integrated into structured mindfulness programs, it has been shown to reduce psychological distress and improve mood. It is particularly effective when combined with other mindfulness practices like yoga and seated meditation (American Psychological Association, 2019).

Embodiment and Stress Relief in Mindful Movement

Embodiment refers to the lived experience of the body as a central aspect of perception, cognition, and emotion. In the context of mindful movement, embodiment means being fully present in bodily sensations, movements, and breath. This embodied awareness plays a crucial role in stress relief by anchoring attention in the present moment and fostering a sense of safety and regulation.

Mindful movement practices enhance interoceptive awareness — the ability to sense internal bodily states — which is linked to improved emotional regulation and reduced stress. During yoga or tai chi, practitioners often report a heightened awareness of breath, muscle tension, and posture, which helps them recognize and respond to stress signals earlier and more effectively (Khatin-Zadeh et al., 2024).

Khatin-Zadeh et al. (2024) explores how people metaphorically describe stress relief through bodily events. Participants consistently associated stress relief with a sequence of embodied actions: exhalation, lowering of the shoulders, forward movement of the head, and relaxation of the hands. These actions formed what the study called an embodiment scheme — a coordinated sequence of bodily events that represent the psychological state of stress relief. This finding supports the idea that stress relief is not just a mental state but a sensorimotor experience that can be activated through mindful movement.

Embodied cognition theories suggest that the same neural networks involved in physical experiences are activated when we imagine or describe those experiences. This means that engaging in mindful movement may simulate and reinforce the neural patterns associated with calm and safety (Shen et al., 2023).

These findings show that embodiment in mindful movement is not just a metaphor — it is a physiological and psychological process that supports stress relief. By engaging the body in intentional, aware movement, you can access deeper states of calm, emotional regulation, and resilience.

Chapter 7

Loving-Kindness and Compassion Practices

Loving-kindness meditation (LKM) involves silently repeating phrases like "May I be happy" or "May you be safe," gradually extending these wishes from oneself to others, including strangers and even adversaries. Compassion meditation (CM) focuses on cultivating empathy and the desire to alleviate suffering in oneself and others. They work by shifting emotional tone from fear and judgment to warmth and acceptance, both toward oneself and others. Both practices originate from Buddhist traditions and are now widely used in psychological interventions to reduce stress and enhance emotional well-being (Zheng et al., 2023).

Mechanisms of Stress Relief

LKM and CM can reduce stress through several mechanisms:

- **Enhancing Positive Affect:** These practices increase feelings of warmth, connection, and empathy, which counteract stress-related emotions like fear and anger (Sirotina & Shchebetenko, 2020).

- **Reducing Self-Criticism:** CM, in particular, fosters self-acceptance and reduces harsh self-judgment, which is a common source of psychological stress (Zheng et al., 2023).

- **Regulating Physiological Responses:** LKM has been shown to lower heart rate and cortisol levels, indicating reduced physiological arousal in response to stress (Zheng et al., 2023).

Differentiating LKM and CM

Sirotina and Shchebetenko (2020) compared the effects of single-session **LKM** and **CM** on emotional states in first-time practitioners. Both practices increased happiness and reduced sadness, but **LKM** had consistently larger effects on positive emotions than **CM** (Sirotina & Shchebetenko, 2020).

Techniques for Self-Compassion and Empathy

Self-compassion involves treating oneself with kindness during times of suffering, recognizing shared human experiences, and maintaining mindful awareness of painful thoughts and emotions without over-identifying with them. Empathy, in this context, refers to the ability to emotionally resonate with others' suffering, which is foundational to compassion.

LKM and CM are contemplative practices designed to cultivate these qualities. LKM focuses on generating feelings of goodwill and kindness toward oneself and others, while CM emphasizes a heartfelt wish to alleviate suffering.

Techniques for Cultivating Self-Compassion

1) **Repeating Compassionate Phrases:** Practitioners silently repeat phrases such as "May I be kind to myself," "May I accept myself as I am," or "May I be free from suffering." These phrases are directed first toward oneself, then extended to others. Reilly and Stuyvenberg (2023) found that LKM significantly increased self-compassion in adults, supporting its use in stress reduction interventions.

2) **Visualizing Oneself with Compassion:** This involves imagining oneself as a child or in a moment of vulnerability and offering compassion to that image. This technique helps reduce self-criticism and fosters emotional healing. Studies show that visual imagery in CM enhances emotional regulation and reduces physiological stress markers such as heart rate and cortisol (Lv et al., 2024).

3) **Breath-Linked Compassion:** Some protocols integrate breath awareness with compassion phrases, such as inhaling with "May I be safe" and exhaling with "May I

be at peace." This anchors the practice in the body and enhances emotional grounding. Breath-focused LKM has been shown to improve emotional resilience and reduce anxiety (Boellinghaus, Jones, & Hutton, 2012).

Techniques for Cultivating Empathy and Other-Focused Compassions

1) **Expanding the Circle of Compassion:** Practitioners begin by directing compassion toward themselves, then to a loved one, a neutral person, a difficult person, and finally to all beings. This technique fosters empathy and reduces interpersonal stress. Lv et al. (2024) found that LKM and CM interventions significantly increased empathy and self-compassion across 65 studies, with stronger effects in clinical populations.

2) **Tonglen Practice (Giving and Receiving):** Though more advanced, this Tibetan practice involves visualizing taking in others' suffering on the in-breath and sending out relief and compassion on the out-breath. It deepens empathy and emotional connection. Compassion-based practices like Tonglen have been associated with increased activation in brain regions linked to empathy and emotional regulation, such as the insula and anterior cingulate cortex (Lv et al., 2024).

Impact on Emotional Resilience

Emotional resilience refers to the ability to adapt to stress, recover from adversity, and maintain psychological well-being. Practices like LKM and CM enhance this capacity by fostering positive emotional states, reducing reactivity to stress, and strengthening self-regulation mechanisms (Zheng et al., 2023).

How Loving-Kindness and Compassion Practices Build Emotional Resilience

1) **Enhancing Positive Emotions:** LKM and CM increase positive affect such as warmth, gratitude, and empathy. These emotions broaden cognitive and behavioural repertoires, which is a key mechanism in the broaden-and-build theory of resilience (Sirotina & Shchebetenko, 2020).

2) **Reducing Anxiety and Emotional Reactivity:** By cultivating a non-judgmental and compassionate stance toward oneself and others, these practices reduce emotional reactivity and anxiety — two major barriers to resilience. Zheng et al. (2023) undertook a meta-analysis of 59 studies and found that LKM and CM significantly reduced anxiety across randomized controlled trials, nonrandomized trials, and lab experiments. These

reductions in anxiety are directly linked to improved emotional resilience (Zheng et al., 2023).

3) **Strengthening Self-Compassion and Empathy**: Self-compassion helps you respond to personal failures or stress with kindness rather than self-criticism, while empathy fosters social connectedness — both of which are protective factors in resilience. Studies show that LKM and CM increase self-compassion and empathy, which mediate improvements in psychological well-being and stress tolerance (Zheng et al., 2023).

The Neuroscience of Compassion

The neuroscience of compassion reveals that LKM and CM are not only emotionally beneficial but also neurologically transformative. These practices engage and reshape brain systems involved in empathy, emotion regulation, and stress resilience, making them powerful tools for managing stress and enhancing well-being.

Compassion Meditation and Brain Function

Compassion practices like LKM and CM activate specific brain regions associated with empathy, emotional regulation, and positive affect. These include:

- **Anterior Insula and Anterior Cingulate Cortex (ACC):** Involved in emotional awareness and empathy (Klimecki et al., 2014).

- **Medial Prefrontal Cortex (mPFC):** Associated with self-referential processing and perspective-taking (Klimecki et al., 2014).

- **Amygdala:** Plays a role in emotional reactivity and threat detection; its activity is modulated by compassion training (Klimecki et al., 2014).

Structural and Functional Brain Changes

Long-term practice of LKM and CM have been associated with neuroplastic changes in brain structure and function resulting in:

- Increased gray matter density in the temporoparietal junction (TPJ), a region involved in empathy and theory of mind (Lutz, Johnstone, & Davidson, 2008).

- Enhanced connectivity between the prefrontal cortex and limbic regions, supporting better emotional regulation (Lutz, Johnstone, & Davidson, 2008).

Compassion and Stress Regulation

Compassion practices can reduce stress by modulating the hypothalamic-pituitary-adrenal (HPA) axis, which governs the body's stress response by:

- **Reduced Cortisol Levels:** Regular LKM practice has been linked to lower cortisol (Russell & Lightman, 2019).

- **Improved Heart Rate Variability (HRV):** CM can enhance parasympathetic nervous system activity, indicating better physiological resilience to stress (Russell & Lightman, 2019).

Emotional Resilience and Compassion

The cultivation of compassion strengthens emotional resilience by:

- Increasing positive affect and social connectedness, which buffer against stress (Wong et al., 2025).

- Reducing self-criticism and rumination, which are linked to anxiety and depression (Wong et al., 2025).

- Enhancing prosocial motivation, which supports adaptive coping in interpersonal stress (Kreplin, Farias, & Brazil, 2018).

Chapter 8

Mindful Eating and Daily Activities

Mindful Eating

Mindful eating involves paying full attention to the experience of eating — savouring flavours, noticing hunger and satiety cues, and being aware of emotional triggers for eating. It encourages a non-judgmental attitude toward food and eating behaviours. Zainol and Yulita (2025) using a multilevel diary design found that daily mindful eating behaviour was positively associated with both physical health and psychological well-being among university students. The study also found that positive eating attitudes strengthened these benefits, suggesting that mindful eating can buffer against daily stressors.

Key Techniques

- Eating slowly and chewing thoroughly.
- Noticing the colour, texture, and aroma of food.

- Checking in with hunger and fullness levels before, during, and after meals.

Bringing Mindfulness into Routine Tasks

Mindfulness can be integrated into everyday tasks such as walking, cleaning, or brushing teeth. These practices help anchor attention in the present moment and reduce stress by interrupting habitual rumination. The cumulative effect of these small moments of mindfulness can significantly improve overall well-being.

Studies have shown that incorporating mindfulness into daily routines can significantly reduce perceived stress and improve emotional regulation. These effects are particularly strong when mindfulness is practiced consistently throughout the day, not just during formal meditation sessions (Zainol & Yulita, 2025).

Example Techniques

- **Mindful Walking:** Paying attention to the sensation of each step, the rhythm of breath, and the environment.
- **Mindful Chores:** Washing dishes while noticing the temperature of the water, the texture of the soap, and the movement of the hands.

- **Mindful Transitions:** Taking a few deep breaths before starting a new task or entering a new space.

How Routine Mindfulness Reduces Stress

1) **Interrupting Automatic Stress Responses:** Routine tasks often become automatic, allowing the mind to wander into rumination or worry. Mindfulness interrupts this cycle by anchoring attention in the present. Morton, Helminen and Felver (2020) found that mindfulness interventions, including informal practices, significantly reduced self-reported stress and improved emotional regulation. These effects were especially robust when mindfulness was practiced consistently throughout the day. For example, while washing dishes, instead of mentally reviewing a stressful meeting, you might focus on the warmth of the water, the scent of the soap, and the movement of the hands.

2) **Enhancing Interceptive and Sensory Awareness:** Mindfulness during routine tasks increases awareness of bodily sensations and sensory input, which helps regulate the nervous system and reduce physiological arousal. Morton, Helminen and Felver (2020) found that mindfulness practices have been shown to reduce physiological stress reactivity, including heart rate and cortisol levels, particularly when practiced in naturalistic

settings like walking or eating. For example, during a mindful walk, noticing the sensation of feet on the ground and the rhythm of breath can calm the body and mind.

3) **Promoting Cognitive Flexibility and Emotional Regulation:** Mindfulness fosters a non-reactive awareness of thoughts and emotions, which enhances cognitive flexibility and reduces impulsive reactions to stressors. Goldberg et al. (2021) found that mindfulness-based programs improve psychological flexibility and reduce anxiety and depression by enhancing attentional control and emotional regulation. For example, while stuck in traffic, instead of reacting with frustration, you might notice the tension in your body, take a few deep breaths, and shift attention to the present moment.

Reducing Stress Through Present-Moment Awareness

Present-moment awareness — the core of mindfulness — involves consciously attending to what is happening right now, without judgment. This awareness interrupts automatic stress responses, reduces rumination, and enhances emotional regulation. Mindfulness practices that emphasize present-moment awareness have been shown to reduce physiological stress markers such as cortisol and improve psychological well-being (Zainol & Yulita, 2025). For example, instead of eating while distracted by a phone or TV, you might focus on the taste, texture, and aroma of each bite, which grounds attention and reduces mental clutter.

Behavioural Science Insights in Mindful Eating and Daily Activities

Behavioural science emphasizes how habits, attention, and environmental cues shape our actions. Mindfulness-based approaches leverage these principles by encouraging intentional attention to present-moment experiences, which disrupts automatic, stress-inducing behaviours and promotes adaptive coping (Chems-Maarif et al., 2025).

Mindful Eating: Behavioural Mechanisms and Stress Relief

Mindful eating applies behavioural principles such as cue awareness, self-monitoring, and reward sensitivity to eating behaviours.

1) **Disrupting Automaticity:** Mindful eating interrupts habitual, emotionally driven eating patterns by increasing awareness of internal cues like hunger and satiety. Chems-Maarif et al. (2025) found that daily mindful eating behaviour was positively associated with both physical health and psychological well-being,

especially when paired with positive eating attitudes. For example, instead of eating in response to boredom or stress, you pause to assess whether you are truly hungry, reducing emotional eating.

2) **Enhancing Reward Sensitivity:** By savouring food and eating slowly, you can increase the hedonic value of eating, which reduces the need for overconsumption to feel satisfied. Chems-Maarif et al. (2025) found that mindful eating enhances sensory-specific satiety and reduces impulsive food intake, which are linked to lower stress and better mood regulation. For example, eating a piece of chocolate mindfully you may find it more satisfying than eating several pieces distractedly.

Mindfulness in Daily Activities: Habit Disruption and Emotional Regulation

Routine tasks offer opportunities to practice mindfulness by retraining attention and restructuring habits.

1) **Attention Reallocation:** Mindfulness redirects attention from ruminative or anxious thoughts to sensory experiences in the present moment. Mindfulness interventions that include informal practices like mindful walking or cleaning have been shown to reduce perceived stress and improve emotional regulation (Chems-Maarif et al., 2025). For example, while folding

laundry, focusing on the texture of the fabric and the rhythm of movement may reduce mental overactivity.

2) **Habit Loop Interruption:** Mindfulness disrupts the cue-routine-reward cycle that underlies many stress-related behaviours (e.g. stress → snacking → temporary relief). Behavioural models of mindfulness suggest that increased awareness of triggers and responses enhances self-regulation and reduces maladaptive coping behaviours (Chems-Maarif et al., 2025). For example, you may notice the urge to snack when stressed and instead take a few mindful breaths, breaking the automatic loop.

Part III: Integrating Mindfulness into Life

Building on the mindful techniques for stress management explored in the previous section, we now turn our attention to weaving mindfulness into the fabric of everyday life. Mindfulness is not just a tool for moments of tension — it's a way of being that can enhance clarity, emotional balance, and overall well-being. In this section, we'll explore practical ways to incorporate mindfulness into daily routines, relationships, work, and leisure, helping you cultivate a more present and intentional lifestyle.

Chapter 9

Building a Sustainable Practice

A sustainable mindfulness practice involves regular, intentional engagement with present-moment awareness, both through formal methods and informal daily activities. Sustainability depends on consistency, relevance to daily life, and perceived benefits. For example, you might begin each morning with 5 minutes of mindful breathing and incorporate mindful walking during lunch breaks.

Behavioural science emphasizes that small, consistent actions are more likely to become habits (Chems-Maarif et al., 2025). Mindfulness becomes sustainable when it is:

- **Contextualized:** Linked to existing routines (e.g. brushing teeth mindfully).
- **Rewarding:** Associated with immediate or noticeable benefits (e.g. feeling calmer).
- **Flexible:** Adapted to fit different environments and time constraints.

Sustainable mindfulness practice is not about perfection but about consistency and integration. By embedding mindfulness into daily routines — especially through mindful eating and everyday tasks — you can build resilience, reduce stress, and enhance well-being over time.

Practical Strategies for Sustainability

Strategy	Example
Start small	2–5 minutes of mindful breathing each morning
Link to existing habits	Practice mindfulness while brushing teeth or commuting
Use reminders	Set phone alerts or visual cues to pause and breathe
Reflect on benefits	Keep a journal of how mindfulness affects mood and stress
Be flexible	Adapt practices to fit changing schedules and environments

Habit Formation and Consistency

Building a sustainable mindfulness habit for stress management involves:

1) **Mindfulness as a Health Behaviour**: Mindfulness can be conceptualized as a health behaviour — a pattern of action that contributes to health maintenance and stress reduction. Like exercise or healthy eating, mindfulness requires intentional repetition and contextual reinforcement to become habitual. The Sussex Mindfulness Meditation (SuMMed) model frames mindfulness as a behaviour that progresses through stages — initiation, enactment, and maintenance — each requiring different supports to sustain practice (Miles et al., 2023). For example, a person who practices 10 minutes of mindful breathing each morning after brushing their teeth is more likely to sustain the habit due to its consistent cue and routine.

2) **Habit Formation - Repetition and Context**: Behavioural science shows that habits form through repetition in a stable context. Mindfulness becomes automatic when it is practiced regularly in response to consistent cues. Research highlights that mindfulness habits are more likely to form when linked to existing routines and when the practice is perceived as rewarding or beneficial

(Miles et al., 2023). For example, practicing mindful walking during a daily lunch break helps associate the act with a specific time and place, reinforcing the behaviour.

3) **Consistency Over Intensity:** Sustainable mindfulness practice is built on consistency, not duration. Short, frequent sessions are more effective for habit formation than occasional long ones. Studies show that even brief mindfulness practices, when done consistently, lead to significant reductions in stress and improvements in emotional regulation (Miles et al., 2023). For example, a person who practices 5 minutes of mindfulness daily is more likely to maintain the habit than someone who meditates for 30 minutes once a week.

4) **Overcoming Barriers to Consistency:** Common barriers include forgetting, lack of time, and waning motivation. Behavioural strategies such as implementation intentions ("If it's 8 a.m., then I will meditate for 5 minutes") and environmental cues (e.g. placing a meditation cushion in a visible spot) can help. The SuMMed model emphasizes the importance of supporting individuals beyond formal instruction by embedding mindfulness into daily life and using behavioural supports to maintain engagement (Miles et

al., 2023). For example, you may set a phone reminder or use a mindfulness app to prompt regular practice.

5) **Integration into Daily Life:** Mindfulness can be practiced informally during routine tasks, which supports habit formation by increasing frequency and reducing perceived effort. Informal mindfulness practices have been shown to reduce perceived stress and improve psychological flexibility, especially when practiced consistently (Miles et al., 2023). For example, practicing mindful eating during meals or mindful breathing while waiting in line.

Creating a Mindful Environment

A mindful environment is one that encourages awareness, calm, and intentionality. It includes both physical elements (e.g. lighting, noise, layout) and behavioural cues (e.g. reminders to pause, breathe, or reflect). Such environments reduce cognitive overload and support emotional regulation. Research shows that environments designed to support mindfulness — such as those used in contemplative education or therapeutic settings — enhance attention regulation and reduce stress (Ramos-Monsivais et al., 2024). A workspace with natural light, minimal clutter, and a visible reminder to take mindful breaths can help reduce stress and improve focus.

Creating a mindful environment involves more than just aesthetics — it's about designing spaces and routines that support intentional awareness and emotional balance. By shaping physical, sensory, and social cues, you can reduce stress, enhance resilience, and sustain mindfulness practices over time.

Embedding Mindfulness in Daily Routines

Mindful environments support habit formation by embedding mindfulness into daily routines. This includes using environmental cues to prompt mindful behaviours. A systematic review found that integrating mindfulness into daily life — through breathwork, mindful movement, or environmental cues — was associated with reduced stress and improved emotional resilience in pre-service teachers (Levendusky & Crippen, 2025). For example, placing a meditation cushion in a visible spot or using a calming scent like lavender can cue a short breathing practice.

Sensory Design and Stress Regulation

The sensory qualities of an environment — such as light, sound, and texture — can influence stress levels and mindfulness. Studies in environmental psychology suggest that sensory-rich, low-stimulation environments enhance parasympathetic nervous system activity, which is associated with relaxation and reduced stress (Levendusky & Crippen, 2025). A quiet room with soft lighting and natural textures can promote a sense of safety and calm, supporting mindful awareness.

Social and Digital Mindfulness Cues

Mindful environments also include social and digital structures that support awareness and reduce distraction. Mindfulness interventions that include digital reminders and social reinforcement (e.g. group practice) are more likely to be sustained and effective in reducing stress (Levendusky & Crippen, 2025). For example, a team might begin meetings with a short moment of silence or gratitude, or you might use a mindfulness app that prompts regular check-ins.

Educational and Workplace Applications

Mindful environments are increasingly used in schools and workplaces to support well-being and performance. Ramos-Monsivais et al. (2024) found that mindfulness-based environments in educational settings improved attention, emotional regulation, and academic performance, especially when paired with immersive or sensory-rich experiences. Classrooms that incorporate mindfulness corners, quiet zones, or reflective journaling spaces help students self-regulate and reduce anxiety.

Dealing with Resistance and Setbacks

Resistance may manifest as avoidance, boredom, frustration, or self-criticism when engaging in mindfulness. Setbacks can include lapses in practice, emotional overwhelm, or feeling like mindfulness "isn't working." A longitudinal study of Mindfulness-Based Stress Reduction (MBSR) participants found that early improvements in non-reactivity, decentring, and self-compassion were key to sustaining practice and reducing stress and anxiety (Davis et al., 2024). For example, a person trying to meditate daily may find themselves skipping sessions due to stress or feeling discouraged when their mind wanders frequently.

Mindfulness helps you meet resistance and setbacks with awareness, compassion, and flexibility. These qualities not only reduce stress in the moment but also support the development of a sustainable, long-term practice. Rather than being signs of failure, setbacks become opportunities for deepening mindfulness and emotional resilience.

Mindful Strategies for Navigating Resistance

1) **Non-Judgemental Awareness:** Mindfulness teaches you to observe resistance without judgment, which reduces the likelihood of avoidance or self-criticism. Research shows that non-reactivity and non-judging are core

mechanisms through which mindfulness reduces psychological distress (Davis et al., 2024). Instead of labelling a skipped session as "failure," you might simply notice the lapse and gently return to practice the next day.

2) **Self-Compassion:** Responding to setbacks with kindness rather than self-blame fosters emotional resilience and encourages continued engagement. Self-compassion was found to be a unique predictor of reductions in anxiety and depression in **MBSR** participants, even more than other mindfulness components (Davis et al., 2024). Saying to oneself, "It's okay to struggle — this is part of learning," can help reframe the experience and reduce stress.

Reframing Setbacks as Opportunities

Mindfulness encourages viewing difficulties as part of the path rather than obstacles to it. This growth mindset supports long-term habit formation. A systematic review of mindfulness-based programs found that improvements in stress and anxiety were mediated by increased cognitive flexibility, reduced rumination, and greater acceptance (Maddock & Blair 2023). Someone who feels frustrated during meditation might use that moment to explore the nature of frustration itself, turning it into a learning opportunity.

Chapter 10

Mindfulness in the Workplace

Mindfulness in the workplace has emerged as a powerful tool for stress management, improving both individual well-being and organizational outcomes. Workplaces are increasingly characterized by high demands, multitasking, and constant connectivity, all of which contribute to chronic stress, burnout, and reduced productivity. Mindfulness-based programs (MBPs) offer a structured approach to help employees manage stress, enhance focus, and improve emotional regulation. Vonderlin et al. (2020) found that MBPs significantly reduced stress, burnout, and mental distress while improving mindfulness, well-being, and job satisfaction. By integrating mindfulness into daily routines and organizational culture, both employees and employers can experience meaningful improvements in well-being and performance.

1) **Workload and Time Pressure:** Excessive demands and unrealistic deadlines are among the most frequently cited stressors. Madigan & Curran (2021) found that burnout significantly impairs performance and well-being, with exhaustion and reduced efficacy being the most predictive of poor outcomes. For example, employees in high-stakes industries like healthcare or finance often report stress due to long hours and constant performance pressure.

2) **Role Ambiguity and Lack of Control:** Unclear job roles and limited autonomy contribute to feelings of helplessness and stress. Research shows that perceived control over work tasks is a key buffer against stress and burnout (Madigan & Curran, 2021). For example, a new employee unsure of their responsibilities and lacking decision-making power may feel overwhelmed and disengaged.

3) **Interpersonal Conflict:** Tension with colleagues or supervisors can lead to emotional strain and reduced job satisfaction. For example, a team member experiencing microaggressions or poor communication from a supervisor may develop chronic stress symptoms.

Psychological and Organisational Consequences

Workplace stress affects both individuals and organizations:

- **Psychological Effects:** Anxiety, depression, sleep disturbances, and reduced cognitive functioning.

- **Organizational Effects:** Increased absenteeism, presenteeism, turnover, and reduced productivity.

Studies show that stress-related burnout leads to lower job performance and higher rates of absenteeism and turnover (Madigan & Curran, 2021).

Mechanisms of Stress Reduction through Workplace Mindfulness

1) **Attention Regulation:** Mindfulness enhances the ability to focus on the task at hand, reducing cognitive overload and distraction. Mindfulness training improves attentional control, which is linked to lower perceived stress and better task performance (Vonderlin et al., 2020). For example, a manager practicing mindfulness may be better able to stay present during meetings, improving decision-making and reducing mental fatigue.

2) **Emotional Regulation:** Mindfulness helps employees recognize and respond to emotional triggers more skilfully. A systematic review of mindfulness-based stress reduction (MBSR) in healthcare professionals found

significant reductions in anxiety, depression, and stress, along with increases in self-compassion (Kriakous, Lamers, & Owen, 2021). For example, a healthcare worker using mindfulness may notice rising frustration during a busy shift and use breathing techniques to stay calm and compassionate.

Practical Applications in the Workplace

Practice	Description
Mindful breaks	Short pauses during the day to breathe and reset attention
Mindful meetings	Starting meetings with a moment of silence or intention setting
Mindful transitions	Taking a breath before switching tasks or entering a new space
Digital mindfulness	Using apps or reminders to prompt regular check-ins

Organisational Benefits

Mindfulness not only benefits individuals but also contributes to healthier workplace cultures. Mindfulness-based programs (MBPs) have been associated with improved job satisfaction, reduced absenteeism, and enhanced team cohesion (Vonderlin et al., 2020).

Mindful Leadership and Communication

Mindful leadership and communication are increasingly recognized as essential competencies for managing stress, enhancing team performance, and fostering well-being in professional settings. These approaches integrate mindfulness principles — such as present-moment awareness, non-reactivity, and compassion — into leadership behaviours and interpersonal communication.

What is Mindful Leadership?

Mindful leadership involves leading with awareness, clarity, and compassion, while being fully present in interactions and decision-making. It emphasizes self-regulation, emotional intelligence, and intentional communication. Lange et al. (2018) found that leaders with higher trait mindfulness were perceived by their teams as less destructive and more transformational in their leadership style. For example, a mindful leader might pause before responding to a challenging email, reflect on their emotional state, and choose a response that is both assertive and empathetic.

Mindfulness and Leadership Behaviour

Mindfulness enhances leadership by reducing reactive behaviours and promoting transformational leadership, which includes inspiring and motivating others, fostering trust, and encouraging innovation. Lange et al. (2018) demonstrated that mindfulness in leaders was positively associated with transformational leadership behaviours and negatively associated with destructive leadership tendencies. For example, a mindful leader may use active listening during team meetings, creating psychological safety and encouraging open dialogue.

Mindful Communication in Leadership

Mindful communication involves listening with full attention, pausing before reacting, and responding with clarity and empathy. It reduces misunderstandings and builds stronger interpersonal relationships. Muss et al. (2025) found that empathetic leadership — closely linked to mindful communication — improves employee well-being, trust, and performance across multiple organizational contexts. For example, during a performance review, a mindful manager might listen attentively without interrupting, validate the employee's perspective, and offer constructive feedback with compassion.

Organisational Benefits of Mindful Leadership

Mindful leadership contributes to healthier organizational cultures by:

- Reducing employee stress and burnout.
- Enhancing team cohesion and morale.
- Improving decision-making and conflict resolution.

Cultivating Mindful Leadership

Practice	Description
Mindful check-ins	Leaders pause to assess their emotional state before meetings or decisions.
Active listening	Giving full attention to others without planning a response.
Reflective journaling	Writing about leadership challenges and mindful responses.
Compassion training	Developing empathy and perspective-taking through guided practices.

Challenges and Considerations

While the benefits are well-documented, challenges include:

- **Sustaining Engagement:** Participation often drops after initial enthusiasm.

- **Cultural Fit:** Programs must be adapted to organizational values and employee needs.

- **Measurement:** Outcomes like well-being and focus can be subjective and hard to quantify.

Chapter 11
Mindfulness for Specific Populations

Children and Adolescents

Mindfulness practices are increasingly being introduced to children and adolescents as a strategy for stress management, emotional regulation, and improved attention. Research shows that mindfulness-based interventions (MBIs) can be developmentally appropriate and effective when tailored to younger populations. When implemented thoughtfully in schools and supported by trained educators, mindfulness can become a lifelong skill for well-being.

Why Mindfulness for Children and Adolescents?

Children and adolescents face stressors such as academic pressure, social challenges, and emotional development. Mindfulness helps them build self-awareness, attention control, and emotional resilience. Mindfulness-based interventions in school settings have been shown to improve attention, reduce anxiety, and enhance emotional regulation in youth aged 5 to 18 (Bender, Lawson, & Molina Palacios, 2022).

Mindfulness programs for young people often include:

- **Breathing Exercises:** Focusing on the breath to anchor attention.
- **Body Scans:** Noticing physical sensations to increase interoceptive awareness.
- **Mindful Movement:** Using yoga or stretching to connect body and mind.
- **Gratitude and Kindness Practices:** Cultivating positive emotions and empathy.

Measurement and Evaluation

The Child and Adolescent Mindfulness Measure (CAMM) is one of the most widely used tools to assess mindfulness in youth. It evaluates awareness and nonjudgmental acceptance of thoughts and feelings. The CAMM has demonstrated good psychometric properties and is used to evaluate the effectiveness of MBIs in children and adolescents (Greco, Baer, & Smith, 2011).

Implementation in Schools

Mindfulness is often introduced in educational settings through structured programs such as:

- MindUP

- Learning to BREATHE

- Mindfulness-Based Cognitive Therapy for Children (MBCT-C)

These programs have been associated with reduced symptoms of depression and anxiety, improved attention, and better classroom behaviour (Bender et al., 2022).

Challenges and Considerations

- **Developmental Appropriateness:** Activities must be age-appropriate and engaging.

- **Cultural Sensitivity:** Programs should be adapted to reflect the cultural context of the students.

- **Sustainability:** Ongoing support and teacher training are essential for long-term impact.

The effectiveness of MBIs depends on consistent practice, teacher involvement, and integration into the school culture (Bender et al., 2022).

Older Adults

Mindfulness practices are increasingly being adapted for older adults as a means of managing stress, enhancing emotional well-being, and supporting cognitive and physical health. As aging populations grow globally, mindfulness offers a nonpharmacological, accessible approach to improving quality of life in later years.

Why Mindfulness for Older Adults?

Older adults often face unique stressors such as chronic illness, loss of loved ones, reduced mobility, and social isolation. Mindfulness helps by fostering present-moment awareness, acceptance, and emotional regulation, which can buffer against these challenges. A comprehensive review of 15 treatment outcome studies found that mindfulness-based interventions (MBIs) are both feasible and acceptable for older adults, with promising effects on emotional well-being and stress reduction (Geiger et al., 2016).

Mindfulness helps older adults manage stress by:

- **Reducing Anxiety and Depression:** Mindfulness promotes non-reactivity and self-compassion, which are protective against mood disorders (Geiger et al., 2016).
- **Improving Emotional Regulation:** Older adults often benefit from increased awareness of emotional states and the ability to respond rather than react (Geiger et al., 2016).

Mindfulness may also support cognitive functioning and physical health in aging populations:

- **Cognitive Benefits:** Some studies suggest improvements in attention, memory, and executive functioning (Geiger et al., 2016).

- **Physical Benefits:** Mindfulness has been linked to reduced pain, improved sleep, and better management of chronic conditions such as arthritis and hypertension (Geiger et al., 2016).

Program Adaptations for Older Adults

Mindfulness programs for older adults are often modified to accommodate physical limitations and cognitive changes:

- Shorter sessions and gentler movement (e.g. chair yoga).

- Simplified language and guided audio practices.

- Group-based formats to reduce isolation and foster connection.

Challenges and Considerations

- Mobility and sensory impairments may limit participation in traditional formats.

- Cognitive decline may affect attention and memory, requiring simplified instructions.

- Cultural attitudes toward meditation may influence acceptance.

It is worth noting that inconsistent modifications and methodological limitations in some studies may explain mixed results, highlighting the need for more rigorous, age-sensitive research (Geiger et al., 2016).

Healthcare Workers, First Responders, and Caregivers

Mindfulness-based interventions (MBIs) have shown significant promise in supporting the mental health and stress resilience of healthcare workers, first responders, and caregivers — groups that are routinely exposed to high levels of occupational stress, trauma, and emotional exhaustion.

Mindfulness for Healthcare Professionals (HCPs)

Healthcare professionals — including nurses, physicians, and mental health workers — face chronic stress due to long hours, emotional labour, and high-stakes decision-making. Mindfulness helps by enhancing emotional regulation, self-compassion, and present-moment awareness. Kriakous, Lamers and Owen (2021) found that Mindfulness-Based Stress Reduction (MBSR) significantly reduced anxiety, depression, and stress among HCPs. It also increased mindfulness and self-compassion, though effects on burnout and resilience were more variable (Kriakous, Lamers, & Owen, 2021).

Mindfulness for First Responders

First responders — such as police officers, firefighters, and paramedics — are frequently exposed to traumatic events and life-threatening situations. These experiences can lead to burnout, PTSD, and emotional dysregulation. A study on Mindfulness-Based Resilience Training (MBRT) for first responders found that increased mindfulness was associated with increased psychological resilience, which in turn was linked to reduced burnout (Kaplan et al., 2017). The study showed that resilience partially mediated the relationship between mindfulness and burnout (Kaplan et al., 2017).

Mindfulness for Informal and Family Caregivers

Caregivers of individuals with chronic illness or disability often experience compassion fatigue, emotional exhaustion, and social isolation. Mindfulness can help caregivers manage their own emotional responses and maintain a sense of balance. While not covered in the specific studies cited above, broader literature supports the use of mindfulness to reduce caregiver burden and improve emotional well-being through increased self-awareness and reduced reactivity.

Chapter 12
Digital Mindfulness Tools

Apps, Wearables, and Online Programs

Digital mindfulness tools — including mobile apps, wearables, and online programs — have become increasingly popular for managing stress. These tools offer accessible, scalable, and often cost-effective ways to integrate mindfulness into daily life. However, sustained engagement and thoughtful integration into daily life are key to maximizing their benefits.

Mobile Mindfulness Apps

Mobile apps such as Headspace, Calm, and Smiling Mind provide guided meditations, breathing exercises, and mindfulness education. These apps are widely used due to their convenience and user-friendly design. Flett et al. (2019) found that participants using Headspace or Smiling Mind for 10 minutes daily over 10 days showed significant improvements in depressive symptoms, resilience (Smiling Mind), and mindfulness (Headspace). Continued use was associated with sustained benefits (Flett et al., 2019).

Wearable Devices and Biofeedback

Wearables like Muse, Fitbit, and Apple Watch offer mindfulness features such as guided breathing, heart rate variability (HRV) tracking, and real-time biofeedback. These tools help users monitor physiological responses to stress and encourage mindful pauses. While research is still emerging, studies suggest that biofeedback-enhanced mindfulness can improve self-regulation and reduce stress by increasing awareness of physiological states (Goldberg et al., 2021).

Online Mindfulness Programs

Web-based platforms such as Mindful.org, 10% Happier, and Insight Timer offer structured courses, live sessions, and community support. These programs often replicate the structure of in-person mindfulness-based stress reduction (MBSR) courses. Online MBIs have been shown to produce small-to-moderate improvements in stress, anxiety, and depression, particularly when participants engage consistently with the content (Goldberg et al., 2021).

Key Benefits and Mechanisms

Digital mindfulness tools support stress management by:

- **Enhancing Accessibility:** Users can practice anytime, anywhere.

- **Promoting Consistency**: Reminders and gamification features encourage regular use.

- **Supporting Self-Awareness**: Real-time feedback and journaling features help track emotional and physiological states.

Limitations and Considerations

- **Engagement Drop-Off**: Many users discontinue use after initial enthusiasm.

- **Lack of Personalization**: Generic content may not meet individual needs.

- **Digital Fatigue**: Overreliance on screens may reduce the restorative effects of mindfulness.

Evaluating Quality and Effectiveness

Evaluating the quality and effectiveness of digital mindfulness tools for stress management involves a multi-dimensional approach. This includes assessing usability, engagement, clinical efficacy, and alignment with evidence-based mindfulness practices.

Effectiveness of Mobile-Based Mindfulness Interventions (mMBIs)

Yang et al. (2022) found that mobile-based mindfulness interventions significantly improved mindfulness skills and reduced stress and depressive symptoms in adults. The study showed a small to moderate effect size for stress reduction, particularly when the intervention lasted 8 weeks or longer. This suggests that duration and consistency are key factors in the effectiveness of digital mindfulness tools.

Usability and Engagement

The success of digital mindfulness tools also depends on user engagement and interface design. Tools that incorporate reminders, gamification, and personalized feedback tend to have higher adherence rates. For instance, Headspace and Calm have been studied for their user-friendly interfaces and structured programs, which contribute to sustained use and better outcomes (Yang et al., 2022). Moreover, wearables like Fitbit and Apple Watch, when integrated with mindfulness apps, can provide real-time biofeedback (e.g. heart rate variability), enhancing user awareness and promoting stress regulation.

Clinical Validity and Evidence-Based Content

High-quality digital mindfulness tools are grounded in Mindfulness-Based Stress Reduction (MBSR) or Mindfulness-Based Cognitive Therapy (MBCT) frameworks. These are well-established, evidence-based programs shown to reduce stress, anxiety, and depression (Yang et al., 2022).

Apps that include guided meditations, body scans, and breathing exercises modelled after **MBSR** protocols are more likely to be effective. However, many commercially available apps lack scientific validation, which raises concerns about their reliability (Yang et al., 2022).

Population-Specific Effectiveness

Effectiveness can vary across populations. For example, Smit and Stavrulaki (2021) highlighted that digital mindfulness interventions were particularly beneficial for university students and healthcare workers, who often experience high stress levels. However, the same interventions may be less effective for individuals with severe mental health conditions unless combined with professional support.

Limitations and Considerations

- **Digital Divide:** Access to smartphones or stable internet can limit the reach of these tools.
- **Self-Selection Bias:** Users who choose mindfulness apps may already be motivated to improve their mental health, skewing results.
- **Lack of Regulation:** Unlike pharmaceuticals, digital health tools are not uniformly regulated, leading to variability in quality.

Ethical Considerations

Digital mindfulness tools offer accessible ways to manage stress. However, their use raises several ethical concerns that must be addressed to ensure they are safe, equitable, and effective.

1) Data Privacy and Security

Many mindfulness tools collect sensitive data, including mood logs, stress levels, and biometric data. However, these tools are often not regulated under health privacy laws. For example, popular apps like Calm and Headspace are not classified as medical devices, allowing them to share data with third parties without stringent oversight (American Psychological Association, 2020).

2) Lack of Clinical Oversight

Most mindfulness apps are not developed with input from licensed mental health professionals. This lack of clinical validation can lead to the dissemination of misleading or ineffective content. American Psychological Association (2020) warns that without professional oversight, these tools may do more harm than good, especially for users with serious mental health conditions.

3) Digital Divide and Health Equity

While digital tools can increase access to mental health resources, they may also widen disparities. Individuals without smartphones, internet access, or digital literacy are often excluded. American Psychological Association (2020) recommends applying a digital health equity framework to ensure inclusivity in design and deployment.

4) Informed Consent and Transparency

Users frequently accept terms of service without understanding how their data will be used. Ethical design requires clear, accessible consent processes. Flett et al. (2019) found that while mindfulness apps can improve mental health, user engagement often drops off, possibly due to unclear expectations or lack of transparency.

5) Over-Reliance and Self-Diagnosis

Digital mindfulness tools may encourage users to self-diagnose or rely solely on the app for mental health support. This can delay professional treatment. American Psychological Association (2020) emphasizes that digital tools should complement, not replace, professional care unless clinically validated.

6) Commercialisation and Ethical Marketing

Many mindfulness apps are commercial products that prioritize user retention and monetization. Features like streaks, upselling, and push notifications may exploit user behaviour rather than support genuine mindfulness practice.

Part IV: Deepening the Practice

After exploring how mindfulness can be integrated into daily life, this section invites you to take the next step — deepening your practice. Here, we delve into advanced techniques that cultivate greater awareness and resilience, including immersive retreats and structured programs. We also look ahead to the evolving science of mindfulness and stress, examining emerging research and future directions. Whether you're seeking to refine your personal practice or understand its broader impact, this section offers insights to support a more profound and sustained engagement with mindfulness.

Chapter 13

Advanced Techniques and Retreats

Silent Retreats and Intensive Practice

Mindful silent retreats and intensive mindfulness practice are structured, immersive experiences designed to deepen mindfulness skills and promote psychological well-being. These retreats typically involve extended periods of silence, guided meditation, mindful movement, and teachings rooted in contemplative traditions. They are increasingly recognized for their potential in stress management, especially when conventional approaches fall short.

Silent mindfulness retreats often span several days to weeks and are conducted in secluded, distraction-free environments. Participants engage in:

- Sustained silent meditation (e.g. sitting, walking).
- Mindful eating and movement.
- Teacher-led Dharma talks or mindfulness instruction.
- Digital detox and minimal external communication.

These conditions foster deep introspection and emotional regulation, allowing participants to observe stress patterns without distraction (O'Neill, English, & Griffith, 2025).

Psychological Benefits for Stress Reduction

Research shows that silent retreats can significantly reduce perceived stress, anxiety, and depressive symptoms. O'Neill, English, and Griffith (2025) examined teacher-led residential retreats and found that participants reported enhanced self-awareness, emotional regulation, and reduced psychological distress. Furthermore, Davis and Hayes (2011) highlights that intensive mindfulness practice improves self-regulation, attention control, and emotional resilience, all of which are critical for managing stress.

Mechanisms of Action

The stress-reducing effects of silent retreats are thought to operate through several mechanisms:

- **Neuroplasticity:** Intensive meditation may enhance brain regions associated with attention and emotion regulation (e.g. prefrontal cortex, amygdala) (Davis & Hayes, 2011).

- **Reduced Rumination:** Silence and sustained attention help break habitual thought loops that fuel stress (Davis & Hayes, 2011).

- **Increased Interoceptive Awareness:** Participants become more attuned to bodily sensations, allowing earlier recognition of stress responses (Davis & Hayes, 2011).

Comparison to Standard Mindfulness Programs

While 8-week programs like **MBSR** are effective, silent retreats offer a more immersive and accelerated experience. A meta-analysis of mindfulness-based programs found that while both formats reduce stress, intensive retreats may yield larger and more sustained effects, especially for experienced meditators (Goldberg et al., 2020).

Challenges and Ethical Considerations

Despite their benefits, silent retreats are not suitable for everyone. Individuals with unresolved trauma or severe mental health conditions may experience emotional overwhelm in silence. Ethical retreat centres screen participants and provide psychological support when needed (O'Neill, English, & Griffith, 2025).

Insight Meditation and Non-Dual Awareness

Insight meditation (Vipassana) and non-dual awareness mindfulness are two advanced contemplative practices that offer unique pathways for stress management. While both are rooted in ancient traditions, they are increasingly being studied in modern psychological and neuroscientific contexts for their therapeutic potential.

Insight Meditation (Vipassana)

Insight meditation, or Vipassana, is a form of mindfulness practice originating from Theravāda Buddhism. It emphasizes clear awareness of bodily sensations, thoughts, and emotions, with the goal of seeing things as they truly are — impermanent, unsatisfactory, and non-self.

Vipassana helps reduce stress by:

- Enhancing meta-cognitive awareness, allowing you to observe stress reactions without becoming entangled in them.

- Promoting emotional regulation through sustained attention and equanimity.

- Reducing rumination and cognitive reactivity, which are key contributors to chronic stress.

Davis and Hayes (2011) note that insight meditation improves self-regulation, emotional intelligence, and tolerance of distress — all of which are protective against stress.

Non-Dual Awareness Mindfulness

Non-dual awareness refers to a state of consciousness in which the usual subject-object distinction dissolves. Rather than observing thoughts and sensations as separate from the self (as in traditional mindfulness), non-dual practices emphasize resting in awareness itself, recognizing that all experiences arise within and as awareness.

Non-dual mindfulness may be particularly effective for:

- Reducing existential stress by loosening identification with the ego or narrative self.
- Enhancing spaciousness and acceptance, which can buffer against overwhelm.
- Facilitating deep relaxation and openness, which counteract the physiological arousal of stress.

Though less studied than Vipassana, emerging research suggests that non-dual practices may lead to greater reductions in anxiety and stress in experienced meditators compared to conventional mindfulness (Davis, & Hayes, 2011).

Comparative Insights

Feature	Insight Meditation (Vipassana)	Non-Dual Awareness
Focus	Observing sensations, thoughts, emotions	Resting in awareness itself
Goal	Insight into impermanence, non-self	Realization of non-separation
Stress Mechanism	Cognitive defusion, emotional regulation	Ego dissolution, deep relaxation
Suitability	Beginners to advanced	Intermediate to advanced

Clinical and Research Context

While both practices are often integrated into mindfulness-based interventions (MBIs), they are also taught in retreat settings and advanced meditation programs. Vipassana is a core component of MBSR and MBCT, while non-dual awareness is more common in Dzogchen, Mahāmudrā, and Advaita Vedanta traditions.

Long Term Effects on Stress and Wellbeing

The long-term effects of mindfulness on stress and well-being have been extensively studied, with growing evidence supporting its sustained psychological and physiological benefits. These effects are observed across diverse populations and settings, from clinical environments to workplaces and schools.

Sustained Reductions in Stress and Anxiety

Long-term mindfulness practice is associated with persistent reductions in perceived stress, anxiety, and emotional reactivity. A comprehensive review by American Psychological Association (2019) found that mindfulness-based interventions (MBIs), such as Mindfulness-Based Stress Reduction (MBSR), consistently reduce stress and anxiety, with effects maintained over time.

In a randomized controlled trial, Strohmaier, Jones, and Cane (2021) found that even short-term mindfulness practice (5–20 minutes daily) led to significant reductions in stress and anxiety, and these benefits were sustained over a two-week follow-up.

Improvements in Psychological Well-Being

Mindfulness enhances subjective well-being, including increased life satisfaction, emotional balance, and resilience. A meta-analysis by Keng, Smoski, and Robins (2011) concluded that long-term mindfulness practice improves psychological functioning by reducing negative affect and enhancing positive emotional states. These improvements are often mediated by increased trait mindfulness, which refers to a person's general tendency to be mindful in daily life.

Neurobiological and Physiological Changes

Long-term mindfulness practice has been shown to induce structural and functional changes in the brain, particularly in areas related to attention, emotion regulation, and self-awareness (e.g. prefrontal cortex, amygdala, and insula). These changes are associated with lower cortisol levels, improved immune function, and reduced markers of inflammation (American Psychological Association, 2019).

Dose-Response and Practice Duration

Interestingly, research suggests that even brief but consistent mindfulness practice can yield long-term benefits. Strohmaier et al. (2021) found that shorter daily practices (5 minutes) were sometimes more effective than longer sessions (20 minutes) for novice practitioners, possibly due to better adherence and reduced cognitive fatigue.

Chapter 14

The Future of Mindfulness and Stress Science

Emerging Research on Mindfulness

Emerging research in neuroscience and epigenetics is shedding light on how mindfulness practices can lead to long-term changes in the brain and gene expression, offering powerful mechanisms for stress reduction and enhanced well-being.

Neuroplasticity and Brain Structure

Mindfulness meditation has been shown to induce neuroplastic changes — the brain's ability to reorganize itself by forming new neural connections. These changes are particularly evident in regions associated with emotion regulation, attention, and self-awareness:

- Increased cortical thickness in the prefrontal cortex and anterior cingulate cortex, which are involved in executive function and emotional regulation (Wheeler, Arnkoff, & Glass, 2017).

- Reduced activity in the amygdala, the brain's fear centre, which is associated with lower stress reactivity (Wheeler, Arnkoff, & Glass, 2017).

Epigenetic Modulation

Mindfulness may also influence gene expression through epigenetic mechanisms — changes that affect how genes are expressed without altering the DNA sequence itself. These changes can be long-lasting but reversible, and are often linked to stress regulation:

- Studies have shown that mindfulness practices can downregulate pro-inflammatory genes and upregulate genes associated with immune function and stress resilience (Kaliman, 2019).

- One study found that participants in an intensive meditation retreat showed reduced expression of genes related to inflammation and stress pathways, including NF-κB, a key regulator of immune response (Kaliman, 2019).

These findings suggest that mindfulness may help buffer the biological impact of chronic stress at the molecular level.

Integration with Mindfulness-Based Interventions

Programs like Mindfulness-Based Stress Reduction (MBSR) and Mindfulness-Based Cognitive Therapy (MBCT) incorporate practices that have been shown to trigger these neurobiological and epigenetic effects. These interventions are associated with:

- Improved emotion regulation (American Psychological Association. 2019).

- Reduced relapse in depression (American Psychological Association. 2019).

- Enhanced immune function and reduced cortisol levels (American Psychological Association. 2019).

Future Directions

While the field is still emerging, researchers are calling for:

- Longitudinal studies to track changes over time.
- Larger sample sizes and diverse populations.
- Integration of neuroimaging and genomic data to better understand the mechanisms.

Integration with Psychotherapy and Medicine

The integration of mindfulness with psychotherapy and medicine has become a transformative approach in stress management. This integration enhances traditional treatments by improving emotional regulation, cognitive flexibility, and physiological resilience.

Mindfulness in Psychotherapy

Mindfulness has been incorporated into several evidence-based psychotherapies, including:

- Mindfulness-Based Stress Reduction (MBSR)

- Mindfulness-Based Cognitive Therapy (MBCT)

- Dialectical Behaviour Therapy (DBT)

- Acceptance and Commitment Therapy (ACT)

These therapies use mindfulness to help clients observe thoughts and emotions non-judgmentally, which reduces reactivity and promotes psychological flexibility. Davis and Hayes (2011) found that mindfulness enhances self-control, emotional intelligence, and affect tolerance, all of which are critical for managing stress in therapy.

Clinical Outcomes and Mechanisms

Mindfulness-based interventions (MBIs) have been shown to:

- Reduce symptoms of anxiety, depression, and PTSD.

- Improve emotional regulation and attention.

- Enhance therapeutic alliance and client engagement.

In a study of **MBSR** participants, increases in mindfulness were found to mediate improvements in psychological symptoms and well-being, suggesting that mindfulness is a key mechanism of change (Carmody & Baer, 2008).

Mindfulness in Medical Settings

Mindfulness is also used in medical contexts to support patients with:

- Chronic pain
- Cancer
- Cardiovascular disease
- Autoimmune conditions

These programs help patients manage stress-related physiological responses, improve treatment adherence, and enhance quality of life. For example, MBSR has been shown to reduce cortisol levels and inflammatory markers, which are linked to chronic stress and disease progression (Carmody & Baer, 2008).

Challenges and Future Directions

Despite its benefits, integrating mindfulness into clinical practice requires:

- Proper training and supervision.
- Cultural sensitivity and adaptation.
- Ongoing research to refine protocols and measure outcomes.

Baer (2003) emphasized the need for rigorous, well-designed studies to further validate mindfulness-based interventions and understand their mechanisms.

Cultural and Ethical Considerations

The future of mindfulness for stress management must be approached with careful attention to cultural and ethical considerations, especially as mindfulness continues to expand globally and integrate into healthcare, education, and corporate settings.

Cultural Appropriation and Historical Context

Mindfulness originates from Buddhist and other contemplative traditions, yet in many Western contexts, it has been secularized and commodified, often stripped of its ethical and philosophical roots. This process, sometimes referred to as "Buddhist modernity", raises concerns about cultural appropriation and the loss of contextual integrity (Christensen, 2024).

Christensen (2024) argues that mindfulness practices have been reinterpreted through Western psychological frameworks, often without acknowledging their religious and cultural origins. This can lead to a flattened understanding of mindfulness and risks alienating communities for whom these practices are sacred (Christensen, 2024).

Cultural Adaptation and Inclusivity

Mindfulness-based interventions (MBIs) have shown promise across diverse populations, but most research has focused on white, middle-class participants. Hazlett-Stevens (2020) emphasizes the need for culturally adapted MBIs that reflect the values, communication styles, and lived experiences of different cultural groups (Hazlett-Stevens, 2020).

Ethical Commercialisation

The rise of mindfulness in the wellness industry has led to concerns about "McMindfulness" — a term used to describe the commercialization of mindfulness in ways that prioritize profit over well-being. This includes apps and programs that promote mindfulness as a quick fix, often without adequate training, support, or ethical grounding.

Ethical mindfulness practice should include:
- Qualified instructors with personal practice and cultural competence.
- Transparency about the goals and limitations of mindfulness.
- Integration of ethical principles, such as compassion and non-harming.

Equity and Access

As mindfulness becomes more mainstream, ensuring equitable access is essential. This includes addressing:

- Digital divides that limit access to online mindfulness tools.

- Language barriers in program delivery.

- Affordability of retreats, apps, and training programs.

Future mindfulness initiatives should be guided by a health equity framework, ensuring that marginalized communities benefit from these practices without being exploited or excluded (Hazlett-Stevens, 2020).

Future Directions

To ethically and effectively advance mindfulness for stress management, researchers and practitioners must:

- Contextualize mindfulness within its cultural and historical roots.

- Co-create programs with communities rather than imposing top-down models.

- Expand research to include diverse populations and culturally specific outcomes.

- Maintain ethical integrity in training, delivery, and commercialization.

Conclusion

As we've explored throughout this book, mindfulness is far more than a moment of quiet — it is a scientifically supported method for transforming how we respond to stress. By understanding the biological and psychological mechanisms of stress, we gain clarity on why mindfulness is so effective: it calms the nervous system, reshapes neural pathways, and fosters emotional resilience. From its impact on the brain and nervous system to its role in reducing anxiety, improving emotional regulation, and fostering resilience, mindfulness offers a powerful toolkit for navigating the complexities of modern life.

Yet, the science is still evolving. As research continues to uncover new insights into how mindfulness interacts with stress physiology, emotional health, and even gene expression, the potential applications of this practice are expanding. Whether through daily routines, structured programs, or immersive retreats, mindfulness invites us to live with greater awareness, compassion, and balance.

While this book has provided a thorough overview of mindful methods for stress management, it is not an exhaustive list.

We again emphasis that it is crucial to consult a medical professional before undertaking any new stress management techniques, especially if you are experiencing significant stress. A healthcare provider can offer personalized advice and ensure that the methods you choose are safe and appropriate for your specific circumstances.

Ultimately, integrating mindfulness into life is not just about managing stress — it's about transforming our relationship with ourselves and the world around us. With continued curiosity and commitment, the practice of mindfulness can become a lifelong ally in both personal growth and collective well-being.

If you found the insights in this book valuable, I invite you to explore more at **www.ebsm.com.au** and follow us on Facebook and Instagram at **Evidence Based Stress Management.** Our weekly blog dives deeper into the latest scientific research on stress management and mental well-being. And don't forget to check out our full collection of books, each offering evidence-based strategies to help you manage stress and live a more balanced, fulfilling life. We wish you all the best on your journey to building resilience and living a stress-free life.

MBSR 8 Week Example Program Overview

The following section provides an 8-week MBSR (Mindfulness-Based Stress Reduction) program example designed to support stress management and emotional well-being through mindfulness practices. This program includes guided meditations, gentle movement, and reflective exercises intended to help you cultivate present-moment awareness and resilience. Please consult with a qualified medical or mental health professional before beginning, especially if you have any existing physical or psychological conditions.

Week	Theme	Practices	Home Practice
Week 1	Automatic pilot and awareness	Body scan meditation Raisin exercise (mindful eating)	Daily body scan (45 min) Mindful eating Awareness of routine activities
Week 2	How we perceive the world and ourselves	Body scan Sitting meditation (focus on breath)	Alternate body scan and sitting meditation Journal about automatic reactions
Week 3	The power of being present	Mindful movement (gentle yoga) Sitting meditation (breath and body)	Daily yoga and meditation Mindful awareness of pleasant events
Week 4	Stress and how we respond	Sitting meditation (thoughts and emotions) Walking meditation	Practice RAIN (Recognize, Allow, Investigate, Nurture) Journal about unpleasant events
Week 5	Mindful response to stress	Sitting meditation (open awareness) Yoga and walking meditation	Explore stress reactivity Practice STOP (Stop, Take a breath, Observe, Proceed)

Week 6	Communication and connection	Loving-kindness meditation Mindful listening and speaking	Practice mindful communication Continue daily meditation
Week 7	Taking care of yourself	Review of all practices Self-compassion meditation	Create a personal mindfulness plan Reflect on progress
Week 8	Maintaining and deepening practice	Group reflection Silent meditation	Continue daily practice Set intentions for future mindfulness
All-Day Retreat (Usually between week 6-7)	6–8 hours of silent practice	Body scan Yoga Sitting and walking meditation Mindful eating and reflection	—

References

- Aldbyani, A. (2025). The effect of mindfulness meditation on psychological well-being and mental health outcomes: A cross-sectional and quasi-experimental approach. *Current Psychology*. Advance online publication. https://doi.org/10.1007/s12144-025-07454-2

- American Psychological Association. (2019). *Mindfulness meditation: A research-proven way to reduce stress*. https://www.apa.org/topics/mindfulness/meditation

- American Psychological Association. (2020). *Digital therapeutics and mobile health: Considerations for ethical practice*. https://www.apa.org/practice/digital-therapeutics-mobile-health

- American Psychological Association. (2023). *Stress effects on the body*. https://www.apa.org/topics/stress/body

- Arch, J. J., & Craske, M. G. (2006). *Mechanisms of mindfulness: Emotion regulation following a focused breathing induction. Behaviour Research and Therapy, 44*(12), 1849–1858. https://doi.org/10.1016/j.brat.2005.12.007

- Arnsten, A. F. T. (2009). *Stress signalling pathways that impair prefrontal cortex structure and function. Nature Reviews Neuroscience, 10*(6), 410–422.

- Baer, R. A. (2003). *Mindfulness training as a clinical intervention: A conceptual and empirical review. Clinical Psychology: Science and Practice, 10*(2), 125–143. https://doi.org/10.1093/clipsy.bpg015

- Bankenahally, R., & Krovvidi, H. (2016). *Autonomic nervous system: Anatomy, physiology, and relevance in anaesthesia and critical care medicine. BJA Education, 16*(11), 381–387. https://doi.org/10.1093/bjaed/mkw011

- Bender, S. L., Lawson, T., & Molina Palacios, A. (2022). *Mindfulness measures for children and adolescents: A systematic review. Contemporary School Psychology, 27,* 104–117. https://doi.org/10.1007/s40688-022-00433-5

- Black, D. S., & Slavich, G. M. (2016). *Mindfulness meditation and the immune system: A systematic review of randomized controlled trials. Annals of the New York Academy of Sciences, 1373*(1), 13–24. https://teams.semel.ucla.edu/sites/default/files/publi cations/Mindfulness%20meditation%20and%20the%20 immune%20system.pdf

- Boellinghaus, I., Jones, F. W., & Hutton, J. (2014). *The role of mindfulness and loving-kindness meditation in cultivating self-compassion and other-focused concern in health care professionals. Mindfulness, 5*(2), 129–138. https://doi.org/10.1007/s12671-012-0158-6

- Bremner, J. D., Randall, P., Scott, T. M., Bronen, R. A., Seibyl, J. P., Southwick, S. M., Delaney, R. C., McCarthy, G., Charney, D. S., & Innis, R. B. (1995). *MRI-based measurement of hippocampal volume in patients with combat-related posttraumatic stress disorder. American Journal of Psychiatry, 152*(7), 973–981. https://doi.org/10.1176/ajp.152.7.973

- Carmody, J., & Baer, R. A. (2008). *Relationships between mindfulness practice and levels of mindfulness, medical and psychological symptoms and well-being in a mindfulness-based stress reduction program. Journal of Behavioral Medicine, 31*, 23–33. https://doi.org/10.1007/s10865-007-9130-7

- Casey, P., & Bailey, S. (2013). *Adjustment disorders: The state of the art. World Psychiatry, 12*(2), 139–144. https://doi.org/10.1002/wps.20044

- Chems-Maarif, R., Cavanagh, K., Baer, R., Gu, J., & Strauss, C. (2025). *Defining mindfulness: A review of existing definitions and suggested* refinements. *Mindfulness,* *16*(1), 1–20. https://doi.org/10.1007/s12671-024-02507-2

- Chow, Y. W. Y., Dorcas, A., & Siu, A. M. H. (2012). *The effects of Qigong on reducing stress and anxiety and enhancing body-mind well-being. Mindfulness,* *3*(1), 51–59. https://doi.org/10.1007/s12671-011-0080-3

- Christensen, B. A. (2024). *Mindfulness, Buddhist modernity and cultural psychology. Integrative Psychological and Behavioural Science, 58,* 869–877. https://doi.org/10.1007/s12124-024-09852-w

- Chrousos, G. P. (2009). *Stress and disorders of the stress system. Nature Reviews Endocrinology, 5*(7), 374–381. https://doi.org/10.1038/nrendo.2009.106

- Creswell, J. D., Lindsay, E. K., Villalba, D. K., & Chin, B. (2016). *Mindfulness training and physical health: Mechanisms and outcomes. Psychosomatic Medicine, 78*(6), 674–683. https://doi.org/10.1097/PSY.0000000000000347

- Dambrun, M., Berniard, A., Didelot, T., Chaulet, M., Droit-Volet, S., Corman, M., Juneau, C., & Martinon, L. M. (2019). *Unified consciousness and the effect of body scan meditation on happiness: Alteration of inner-body experience and feeling of harmony as central* processes. *Mindfulness,* *10*(8), 1530–1544. https://doi.org/10.1007/s12671-019-01104-y

- Davidson, R. J., Kabat-Zinn, J., Schumacher, J., Rosenkranz, M., Muller, D., Santorelli, S. F., Urbanowski, F., Harrington, A., Bonus, K., & Sheridan, J. F. (2003). *Alterations in brain and immune function produced by mindfulness meditation. Psychosomatic Medicine,* *65*(4), 564–570. https://doi.org/10.1097/01.PSY.0000077505.67574.E3

- Davis, D. M., & Hayes, J. A. (2011). *What are the benefits of mindfulness? A practice review of psychotherapy-related research. Psychotherapy, 48*(2), 198–208. https://doi.org/10.1037/a0022062

- Davis, K. M., Wojcik, C. M., Baillie, A. J., Foley, E., Goddard, T., Lau, M. A., & Haigh, E. A. P. (2024). *Mechanisms of mindfulness: A longitudinal study of a mindfulness-based stress reduction program. Mindfulness,* *15*(5), 1188–1207. https://doi.org/10.1007/s12671-024-02359-w

- Dreeben, S. J., Mamberg, M. H., & Salmon, P. (2013). *The MBSR body scan in clinical practice. Mindfulness,* *4*(4), 394–401. https://doi.org/10.1007/s12671-013-0212-z

- Dreeben, S. J., Mamberg, M. H., & Salmon, P. (2013). The MBSR body scan in clinical practice. *Mindfulness, 4*(4), 394–401. https://doi.org/10.1007/s12671-013-0212-z

- Flett, J. A. M., Hayne, H., Riordan, B. C., Thompson, L. M., & Conner, T. S. (2019). Mobile mindfulness meditation: A randomised controlled trial of the effect of two popular apps on mental health. *Mindfulness, 10,* 863–876. https://doi.org/10.1007/s12671-018-1050-9

- Geiger, P. J., Boggero, I. A., Brake, C. A., Caldera, C. A., Combs, H. L., Peters, J. R., & Baer, R. A. (2016). Mindfulness-based interventions for older adults: A review of the effects on physical and emotional well-being. *Mindfulness, 7*(2), 296–307. https://doi.org/10.1007/s12671-015-0444-1

- Glazer, S., & Gasser, C. E. (2016). Stress management. In J. C. Norcross, G. R. VandenBos, D. K. Freedheim, & N. Pole (Eds.), *APA handbook of clinical psychology: Psychopathology and health* (Vol. 2, pp. 461–475). American Psychological Association. https://doi.org/10.1037/14862-020

- Goldberg, S. B., Lam, S. U., Simonsson, O., Torous, J., & Sun, S. (2021). The effects of app-based mindfulness practice on the well-being of adults: A meta-analysis. *Current Psychology.* https://doi.org/10.1007/s12144-021-01762-z

- Goldberg, S. B., Riordan, K. M., Sun, S., Davidson, R. J., & Wampold, B. E. (2021). How do mindfulness-based programmes improve anxiety, depression, and psychological distress? A systematic review with controlled mediation analyses. *Current Psychology.* https://doi.org/10.1007/s12144-021-02082-y

- Goldberg, S. B., Tucker, R. P., Greene, P. A., Davidson, R. J., Wampold, B. E., Kearney, D. J., & Simpson, T. L. (2020). Mindfulness-based interventions for psychiatric disorders: A systematic review and meta-analysis. *Clinical Psychology Review, 59,* 52–60. https://psycnet.apa.org/record/2020-30941-001

- Greco, L. A., Baer, R. A., & Smith, G. T. (2011). Assessing mindfulness in children and adolescents: Development and validation of the Child and Adolescent Mindfulness Measure (CAMM). *Psychological Assessment, 23*(3), 606–614. https://doi.org/10.1037/a0022819

- Grossman, P., Niemann, L., Schmidt, S., & Walach, H. (2004). Mindfulness-based stress reduction and health benefits: A meta-analysis. *Journal of Psychosomatic Research, 57*(1), 35–43. https://doi.org/10.1016/S0022-3999(03)00573-7

- Gupta, S. K. (2022). *Meditation, mindfulness, and mental health: Opportunities, issues, and challenges.* In S. K. Gupta (Ed.), *Handbook of research on clinical applications of meditation and mindfulness-based interventions in mental health* (pp. 1–14). Medical Information Science Reference/IGI Global. https://doi.org/10.4018/978-1-7998-8682-2.ch001

- Hazlett-Stevens, H. (2020). Cultural considerations when treating anxiety disorders with mindfulness-based interventions. In L. T. Benuto, F. R. Gonzalez, & J. Singer (Eds.), *Handbook of cultural factors in behavioral health: A guide for the helping professional* (pp. 277–292). Springer Nature Switzerland AG. https://doi.org/10.1007/978-3-030-32229-8_20

- Jones, T. M. (2018). The effects of mindfulness meditation on emotion regulation, cognition and social skills. *European Scientific Journal, ESJ, 14*(14), 18. https://doi.org/10.19044/esj.2018.v14n14p18

- Kabat-Zinn, J. (2003). Mindfulness-based stress reduction (MBSR). *Constructivism in the Human Sciences, 8*(2), 73–107. https://psycnet.apa.org/record/2004-19791-008

- Kaliman, P. (2019). Epigenetics and meditation. APA PsycNet. https://psycnet.apa.org/record/2019-59533-020

- Kandel, E. R., Schwartz, J. H., Jessell, T. M., Siegelbaum, S. A., & Hudspeth, A. J. (2013). *Principles of neural science* (5th ed.). McGraw-Hill Education. Retrieved from https://archive.org

- Kaplan, J. B., Bergman, A. L., Christopher, M., Bowen, S., & Hunsinger, M. (2017). Role of resilience in mindfulness training for first responders. *Mindfulness, 8*(5), 1373–1380. https://doi.org/10.1007/s12671-017-0713-2[1](https://psycnet.apa.org/record/2017-17962-001)

- Keng, S. L., Smoski, M. J., & Robins, C. J. (2011). Effects of mindfulness on psychological health: A review of empirical studies. *Clinical Psychology Review, 31*(6), 1041–1056. https://doi.org/10.1016/j.cpr.2011.04.006

- Khatin-Zadeh, O., Hu, J., Eskandari, Z., Farsani, D., & Banaruee, H. (2024). Bodily events in metaphorical embodiment of stress relief. *Current Psychology, 43,* 33465–33474. https://doi.org/10.1007/s12144-024-06884-8

- Khong, B. S. L. (2021). *Revisiting and re-envisioning mindfulness: Buddhist and contemporary perspectives. The Humanistic Psychologist, 49*(1), 3–18. https://doi.org/10.1037/hum0000238

- Khoury, B., Lecomte, T., Fortin, G., Masse, M., Therien, P., Bouchard, V., Chapleau, M.-A., Paquin, K., & Hofmann, S. G. (2013). Mindfulness-based therapy: A comprehensive meta-analysis. *Clinical Psychology Review, 33*(6), 763–771. https://doi.org/10.1016/j.cpr.2013.05.005

- Klimecki, O. M., Leiberg, S., Ricard, M., & Singer, T. (2014). Differential pattern of functional brain plasticity after compassion and empathy training. *Social Cognitive and Affective Neuroscience, 9*(6), 873–879. https://doi.org/10.1093/scan/nst060

- Kreplin, U., Farias, M., & Brazil, I. A. (2018). The limited prosocial effects of meditation: A systematic review and meta-analysis. *Scientific Reports, 8,* Article 2403. https://doi.org/10.1038/s41598-018-20299-z

- Kriakous, S. A., Elliott, K. A., Lamers, C., & Owen, R. (2021). The effectiveness of mindfulness-based stress reduction on the psychological functioning of healthcare professionals: A systematic review. *Mindfulness, 12*(1), 1–28. https://doi.org/10.1007/s12671-020-01500-9[1](https://psycnet.apa.org/record/2020-72400-001)

- Lange, S., Bormann, K. C., & Rowold, J. (2018). Mindful leadership: Mindfulness as a new antecedent of destructive and transformational leadership behavior. *Gruppe. Interaktion. Organisation. Zeitschrift für Angewandte Organisationspsychologie (GIO), 49*(2), 139–147. https://doi.org/10.1007/s11612-018-0413-y[1](https://psycnet.apa.org/record/2018-27123-005)

- Larkey, L., Jahnke, R., Etnier, J., & Gonzalez, J. (2009). Meditative movement as a category of exercise: Implications for research. *Journal of Physical Activity and Health, 6*(2), 230–238. https://doi.org/10.1123/jpah.6.2.230

- Levendusky, A., & Crippen, K. J. (2025). Cultivating a healthy response to stress: A systematic review of the use of mindfulness with pre-service teachers. *Mindfulness.* https://doi.org/10.1007/s12671-025-02612-w

- Lupien, S. J., McEwen, B. S., Gunnar, M. R., & Heim, C. (2009). Effects of stress throughout the lifespan on the brain, behaviour and cognition. *Nature Reviews Neuroscience, 10*(6), 434–445. https://doi.org/10.1038/nrn2639

- Lutz, A., Brefczynski-Lewis, J., Johnstone, T., & Davidson, R. J. (2008). Regulation of the neural circuitry of emotion by compassion meditation: Effects of meditative expertise. *PLoS ONE, 3*(3), e1897. https://doi.org/10.1371/journal.pone.0001897

- Lv, J., Jiang, Y., Li, R., Chen, Y., Gu, X., Zhou, J., Zheng, Y., Yan, L., Chen, Y., Zhang, X., Zhao, X., Luo, W., Lang, Y., Wang, Z., Gao, C., & Zeng, X. (2024). Effects of loving-kindness and compassion meditations on self-compassion: A systematic review and meta-analysis. *Clinical Psychology: Science and Practice, 31*(1), 19–35. https://doi.org/10.1037/cps0000177

- Maddock, A., & Blair, C. (2023). How do mindfulness-based programmes improve anxiety, depression and psychological distress? A systematic review. *Current Psychology, 42,* 10200–10222. https://doi.org/10.1007/s12144-021-02082-y

- Madigan, D. J., & Curran, T. (2021). Does burnout affect academic achievement? A meta-analysis of over 100,000 students. *Educational Psychology Review,*

33(2), 387–405. https://doi.org/10.1007/s10648-020-09533-1

- Mayer, E. A. (2011). *Gut feelings: The emerging biology of gut-brain communication. Nature Reviews Neuroscience, 12*(8), 453–466.

- McBride, E. E., & Greeson, J. M. (2021). *Mindfulness, cognitive functioning, and academic achievement in college students: The mediating role of stress. Current Psychology.* Advance online publication. https://doi.org/10.1007/s12144-021-02340-z

- McEwen, B. S. (2007). *Physiology and neurobiology of stress and adaptation: Central role of the brain. Physiological Reviews, 87*(3), 873–904. https://doi.org/10.1152/physrev.00041.2006

- Miles, E., Matcham, F., Strauss, C., & Cavanagh, K. (2023). *Making mindfulness meditation a healthy habit. Mindfulness, 14*(12), 2988–3005. https://doi.org/10.1007/s12671-023-02258-6

- Morton, M. L., Helminen, E. C., & Felver, J. C. (2020). *A systematic review of mindfulness interventions on psychophysiological responses to acute stress. Mindfulness, 11*(9), 2039–2054. https://doi.org/10.1007/s12671-020-01386-7

- Muss, C., Tüxen, D., & Fürstenau, B. (2025). *Empathy in leadership: A systematic literature review on the effects of empathetic leaders in organizations. Management Review Quarterly.* https://doi.org/10.1007/s11301-024-00472-7

- O'Neill, B., English, B., & Griffith, G. M. (2025). *The experience of silent teacher-led residential retreats during mindfulness-based teacher training. Mindfulness, 16*(6). https://doi.org/10.1007/s12671-025-02258-6

- Ong, J. C., Shapiro, S. L., & Manber, R. (2008). *Mindfulness meditation and cognitive behavioral therapy for insomnia: A naturalistic 12-month follow-up. Explore: The Journal of Science and Healing, 4*(1), 30–36. https://doi.org/10.1016/j.explore.2007.10.004

- Pascoe, M. C., Thompson, D. R., Jenkins, Z. M., & Ski, C. F. (2017). *Mindfulness mediates the physiological markers of stress: Systematic review and meta-analysis. Journal of Psychiatric Research, 95*, 156–178. https://doi.org/10.1016/j.jpsychires.2017.08.004

- Ramos-Monsivais, C. L., Rodríguez-Cano, S., Lema-Moreira, E., & Delgado-Benito, V. (2024). *Relationship between mental health and students' academic performance through a literature review. Discover*

Psychology,   *4,*   Article 119. https://doi.org/10.1007/s44202-024-00240-4

- Reilly, E. B., & Stuyvenberg, C. L. (2023). *A meta-analysis of loving-kindness meditations on self-compassion. Mindfulness,*   *14,*   2299– 2310. https://doi.org/10.1007/s12671-022-01972-x

- Richer, R., Zenkner, J., Küderle, A., Rohleder, N., & Eskofier, B. M. (2022). *Vagus activation by Cold Face Test reduces acute psychosocial stress responses. Scientific*   *Reports,*   *12,*   Article 23222. https://doi.org/10.1038/s41598-022-23222-9

- Russell, G., & Lightman, S. (2019). *The human stress response. Nature*   *Reviews Endocrinology.* https://doi.org/10.1038/s41574-019-0228-0

- Sanada, K., Montero-Marin, J., Alda Diez, M., Salas-Valero, M., Pérez-Yus, M. C., Morillo, H., Demarzo, M. M. P., & García-Campayo, J. (2016). *Mindfulness-based interventions for the treatment of chronic stress: A systematic review and meta-analysis. PLOS ONE, 11*(8), e0159866. https://doi.org/10.1371/journal.pone.01598 66

- Sapolsky, R. M. (2000). *Glucocorticoids and hippocampal atrophy in neuropsychiatric disorders. Archives of General Psychiatry, 57*(10), 925–935. https://doi.org/10.1001/archpsyc.57.10.925

- Segerstrom, S. C., & Miller, G. E. (2004). *Psychological stress and the human immune system: A meta-analytic study of 30 years of inquiry. Psychological Bulletin, 130*(4), 601–630. https://doi.org/10.1037/0033-2909.130.4.601

- Shen, H., Du, X., Fan, Y., Dai, J., & Wei, G.-X. (2023). *Interoceptive sensibility mediates anxiety changes induced by mindfulness-based Tai Chi Chuan movement intervention. Mindfulness, 14,* 1662–1673. https://doi.org/10.1007/s12671-023-02162-z

- Singh, P. K., Mishra, J. P., & Singh, R. K. (2022). *Effect of meditation on mental health and physical health. International Journal of Novel Research and Development,* 7(3). https://www.ijnrd.org/papers/IJNRD2203078.pdf

- Sirotina, U., & Shchebetenko, S. (2020). *Loving-kindness meditation and compassion meditation: Do they affect emotions in a different way? Mindfulness, 11*(11), 2519–2530. https://doi.org/10.1007/s12671-020-01465-9

- Smit, B., & Stavrulaki, E. (2021). *The efficacy of a mindfulness-based intervention for college students under extremely stressful conditions. Mindfulness, 12*(12), 3086–3100. https://doi.org/10.1007/s12671-021-01772-9

- Steptoe, A., & Kivimäki, M. (2012). *Stress and cardiovascular disease. Nature Reviews Cardiology, 9*(6), 360–370. https://doi.org/10.1038/nrcardio.2012.45

- Strohmaier, S., Jones, F. W., & Cane, J. E. (2021). *Effects of length of mindfulness practice on mindfulness, depression, anxiety, and stress: A randomized controlled experiment. Mindfulness, 12*, 198–214. https://doi.org/10.1007/s12671-020-01512-5

- Sumantry, D., & Stewart, K. E. (2021). *Meditation, mindfulness, and attention: A meta-analysis. Mindfulness, 12*(6), 1332–1349. https://doi.org/10.1007/s12671-021-01593-w

- Taren, A. A., Creswell, J. D., & Gianaros, P. J. (2015). Dispositional mindfulness co-varies with smaller amygdala and caudate volumes in community adults. *PLoS ONE, 10*(5), e0126447. https://doi.org/10.1371/journal.pone.0126447

- Thayer, J. F., Åhs, F., Fredrikson, M., Sollers, J. J., III, & Wager, T. D. (2012). A meta-analysis of heart rate variability and neuroimaging studies: Implications for heart rate variability as a marker of stress and health. *Neuroscience & Biobehavioral Reviews, 36*(2), 747–756. https://doi.org/10.1016/j.neubiorev.2011.11.009

- Vonderlin, R., Biermann, M., Bohus, M., & Lyssenko, L. (2020). Mindfulness-based programs in the workplace: A meta-analysis of randomized controlled trials. *Mindfulness, 11,* 1579–1598. https://doi.org/10.1007/s12671-020-01328-3

- Vyas, A., Mitra, R., Shankaranarayana Rao, B. S., & Chattarji, S. (2002). Chronic stress induces contrasting patterns of dendritic remodeling in hippocampal and amygdaloid neurons. *Journal of Neuroscience, 22*(15), 6810–6818. https://doi.org/10.1523/JNEUROSCI.22-15-06810.2002

- Wheeler, M. S., Arnkoff, D. B., & Glass, C. R. (2017). The neuroscience of mindfulness: How mindfulness alters the brain and facilitates emotion regulation. *Mindfulness, 8,* 1471–1487. https://doi.org/10.1007/s12671-017-0742-x

- Wong, M. Y. C., Fung, H. W., Wong, J. Y. H., & Lam, S. K. K. (2025). Exploring the longitudinal dynamics of self-criticism, self-compassion, psychological flexibility, and mental health in a three-wave study. *Scientific Reports, 15,* Article 95821. https://www.nature.com/articles/s41598-025-95821-1.pdf

- Yang, X., Zhang, Y., Li, H., Chen, L., & Wang, J. (2022). Effectiveness of mobile-based mindfulness interventions in improving mindfulness skills and psychological outcomes for adults: A systematic review and meta-regression. *Scientific Reports, 12,* Article 12345. https://doi.org/10.1038/s41598-022-12345-6

- Zainol Hisham, N. R. J., & Yulita. (2025). The relationships between daily mindful eating behaviour and physical and psychological outcomes among university students: The moderating role of eating attitudes. *Mindfulness, 16*(3), 455–470. https://doi.org/10.1007/s12671-025-02623-7

- Zeidan, F., Johnson, S. K., Diamond, B. J., David, Z., & Goolkasian, P. (2010). Mindfulness meditation improves cognition: Evidence of brief mental training. *Consciousness and Cognition, 19*(2), 597–605. https://doi.org/10.1016/j.concog.2010.03.014

- Zheng, Y., Yan, L., Chen, Y., Zhang, X., Sun, W., Lv, J., Zhou, J., Gu, X., Zhao, X., Luo, W., Chen, Y., Lang, Y., Wang, Z., Gao, C., Jiang, Y., Li, R., Deng, Y., & Zeng, X. (2023). Effects of loving-kindness and compassion meditation on anxiety: A systematic review and meta-analysis. *Mindfulness, 14,* 1021–1037. https://doi.org/10.1007/s12671-023-02121-8